ODD ASPECTS OF ENGLAND

Odd Aspects of England

by GARRY HOGG

ARCO PUBLISHING COMPANY, INC.
New York

Published by ARCO PUBLISHING COMPANY, Inc.
219 Park Avenue South, New York, N.Y. 10003

Library of Congress Catalog Card Number 69-17312

Arco Book Number 668-01908-5

Printed in Great Britain

Contents

Author's Foreword

'The world is so full of a number of things,' wrote Robert Louis Stevenson, 'I'm sure we should all be as happy as kings.' Substitute 'England' for 'world' (for after all, this relatively small country may be said to be a microcosm) and the comment is apt enough. The days when kings could claim to be happy —if indeed there ever were such days, outside the realm of fairyland—may well be said to have passed; uneasy still, as ever, lies the head that wears a crown.

But the owner of a camera, footloose-and-fancy-free in England (or Scotland, Wales, or Ireland, for that matter) has every reason to feel himself monarch of all that he and his camera survey: there is so much, and in variety so abundant, to be tracked down, considered, and placed on record, whether in colour or in black-and-white. As one such, I have enormously enjoyed two or three months of driving some nine thousand miles about the country, from Land's End to the Scottish Border and from the East Anglian coast to the Welsh Marches, cameras at the ready, in search of the unusual, the picturesque, the unexpected-but-rewarding, the amusing, the memorable—even the disillusioning Odd Aspects of England.

Not that I often encountered the last-named; in fact, this category was satisfyingly rare. But in this connection I had to bear in mind that what afforded me interest or pleasure might merely prove a disappointment to someone else. It was with this in mind that, rather than limit the number of individual subjects to the actual number of pages available, I have in many cases grouped several to a page: subjects that possess something in common, of course, in every case. By so doing, I have been able to throw the net a little wider than would have been possible otherwise. Out of the five-hundred-odd photographs that I took I have included about a hundred, with a dozen or so from other sources for a variety of reasons. In addition to the pictures and the matching text I have referred to a considerable number of alternatives in the twelve categories, which have not been illustrated or dealt with in detail. And of course there are many hundreds more to which no reference at all has been made, and which are, so to speak, wide open to the enterprising camera-equipped enthusiast for out-of-the-way material such as this.

Exception may well be taken to headings for the subjects I have selected, and also to some of the items included under those headings. Perhaps bridge oratories, and windmills likewise, should have been listed under Buildings;

the Minack Theatre under Natural Features. Some of the Follies should perhaps have been listed as Memorials; some of the Memorials under Medieval. The Roman pharos should perhaps have been entered as a Building; and the Long Man of Wilmington not under Oddments but under Prehistoric. But the permutations and combinations are limitless and offer scope for argument and ingenuity one way and another.

In fact, though—does it really matter all that much? I thought not, when I came to sort through the host of illustrations I had assembled for the book. Certain categories at once stood out from the remainder: Prehistoric, Roman, Medieval. Follies and Windmills, too. The range within each category inevitably reflects my own basic interests: Bridges and Follies appealed to me more than did Turf-cut Figures, and this last category was eventually abandoned (though a place had to be found for Wilmington's Long Man!). Windmills appealed to me more than church Round Towers, and eventually this category too was omitted—though there is much of interest and profit to be found in their locating and evaluating, camera in hand. You may well find your own preferences in sharp contradistinction to my own, as revealed here. Well, if this is the case then the remedy lies to your hand. A few hundred miles of judicious driving, with a large-scale map available as well as your camera, and you will soon have restored the balance to your own satisfaction, and have produced the raw material of a more comprehensive book than this can truly claim to be; for it is designed primarily not so much to satisfy as to stimulate interest in an inexhaustible field.

G.H.

Groombridge
Sussex

1 FOLLIES

KNOWN ALSO as Eye-Catchers, Prospect-Towers, Sham Ruins and by other names, these are to be found widely distributed throughout England: something like two hundred have been listed and can be pin-pointed without difficulty on any medium-scale map. It has been said that 'the mark of the true Folly is that it was erected to satisfy its builder and greatly to surprise the stranger'. The Folly may also be said to have been a 'status symbol'. The heyday of Folly building was the eighteenth century, but there are many examples of earlier Follies, and some later. No two are alike; all are well worth hunting down and examining for their eccentricity and unexpectedness.

May's Folly, Hadlow, Kent, three miles north-east of Tonbridge. This example dates only from 1840, a spectacularly tall octagonal building of pseudo-Gothic style leaping skywards from the remains of the Gothic-revival 'Castle' built by Squire May in a fit of extravagant fancy. The conventional refer to it as a 'monument to the tastelessness of its architect'; probably they are right. But though grotesque, like the camel or giraffe it possesses a certain unexpected and illogical dignity of its own. The castellated circular turret clings engagingly to it for half its height.

Why was it built? There are several stories. One is that May wanted to be able to see the sea from Hadlow (an impossibility). Another that he wanted the erring wife who had deserted him for a Kent farmer to be reminded of his existence wherever she might go and live. A third, that he wanted, when he died, to be buried 'above ground, high enough to be able to keep an eye all over his demesnes'. You may take your pick, or even produce a variant of your own. But even if you find nothing but grotesqueness in the tower, there are others who are happy to live in its shadow. The remains of the Castle he built for himself consist of little more than a range of stabling and well-constructed outbuildings, clustered about the tower's foot; and these have been skilfully re-organised into dwellings on a modest scale, homelier by far than the Castle can ever have been. They share the spacious lawn and gardens contained within a ha-ha which divides them from the wide-spreading pastureland of this peaceful corner of Kent, well named the Garden of England.

Triangular Lodge, Rushton, Northants, three miles north-west of Kettering. Older by two centuries and a half, and earlier by a great deal than the majority of England's Follies, this extraordinary building was erected in the year 1595 by Sir Thomas Tresham, an ardent Catholic with an admitted obsession about The Trinity. This is symbolised by the prevalence of the figure three, and multiples thereof. It has in fact been described as 'an essay in stone arithmetic'.

The Lodge, which stands on a smooth lawn set about with conifers and protected by a high stone wall, is, as its name implies, three-sided. But this is only the beginning. Each of the three sides is 33 feet 3 inches long and each corner an exact 60 degrees. There are three floors, each having three triangular windows in each of its three walls. The rooms are either three-sided or six-sided. There are three triangular gables to each of the three sides, nine in all, with triple pinnacles above.

The Lodge is built in yellow-brownish stone, and here for once Sir Thomas had to abandon his obsession: the builder he employed not unnaturally refused to build with triangular blocks! As to decoration: there are trefoil mouldings pierced by triangular holes; the cruciform arrow-slits have pierced trefoils, and the upper range of them are differently shaped each from the other, all nine of them. The gargoyles, as might be anticipated in view of this strange obsession of the designer of this Folly, number nine. Inevitably, of course, there are a number of appropriate inscriptions, and these, in view of the distinction of Sir Thomas, his overpowering concern with The Trinity, and the age in which he lived and moved, are done in Latin. But not just casually. They appear in double-three couplets, each phrase consisting of exactly thirty-three letters. Boldly inscribed on the wall that confronts you as you approach across the greensward beneath the trees are two figures: 3, and 9, or triple-three. No one could call the Lodge beautiful, or even charming, in spite of its gracious setting; it is, it must be confessed, something of a monstrosity. It may be in a better state of repair than that other triangular Folly, Haldon Belvedere, in Devonshire, but it is less imposing, 'mathematical architecture' merely, let us say.

Haldon Belvedere, Doddiscombsleigh, Devon, off A38, five miles south-west of Exeter. Visible from many miles around, it dominates the skyline but is difficult to locate without local instructions, for these are 'lost' Devonshire lanes. You must ask for 'Lawrence Castle', its local name. Why so? Because it was built, in 1788, by Sir Robert Palk, ex-Governor of Madras, for his close friend Major-General Stringer Lawrence, who is commemorated there in three tablets in the hall. Further evidence of the close association with India lies in the fact that the material of the staircases was Indian marble presented by the Nizam of Hyderabad, an admirer also.

Situated on the top of a tree-clad hill, at a height of some eight hundred feet above sea-level, the Belvedere (yet another name for a Prospect-Tower) rises seventy feet through three floors, with a massive round tower marking each of the three corners. The towers, like the main building, are lit by Gothic-arched windows up to the third storey; their crenellated battlements rise higher than the main building, with arrow-slits in them, more for decoration than for use.

It is occupied today—unlike the great majority of Follies. When the occupants are in residence you may, for a very modest fee, enter and look around. Note the remarkably beautiful mahogany floor in the so-called ball-room (the place is much larger than you might suppose from a casual glance at the exterior). Note the rose-centred ceiling, the interesting colour of the walls within, and the dark blue and white ornamentation of the staircase. It is on the first floor that you will come to the ballroom, where you may be told that the mahogany composing the floor came from the East Indies after an altercation with the French who were at that time its owners. Above all, when you have climbed as high as you are permitted to go, make sure that you take the opportunity to look out from each window in turn: the view is magnificent, wherever you look, especially eastwards over the gleaming estuary of the River Exe, flowing down from the high moorland by way of Exeter to the sea. You may have been grumbling about the difficulty of actually reaching a Folly so clearly seen from afar; but you must admit, now, that you have been rewarded.

Sugar Loaf, Dallington, Sussex, five miles north-west of Battle. Known also as Mad Jack Fuller's Folly, it was built by a Sussex eccentric early in the nineteenth century (he died in 1834) as the result of a wager. His friends challenged his statement that he could see the spire of Dallington Church from his home in Brightling Park, and he was proved wrong. Known as 'Honest Jack', he duly paid up; then, to satisfy a whim, caused an exact replica of Dallington spire to be built by the roadside at Woods Corner, so situated that from his window it appeared to be rising from the ridge carrying the road (B2096). 'At least I can see it now,' he said; 'and no one can tell one from t'other.' In general terms he was right in this.

The building stands about forty feet in height, tapering to a point. Inside is a beaten-earth floor some fourteen feet in diameter. Peripheral sockets eight feet up reveal where an upper floor was supported on joists (though it must have been attained by ladder and trap-door). In fact, this odd building was used as a cottage as recently as 1880; it must have been a comfortless place, having neither fireplace nor chimney. Its narrow entrance faces north-east; its sole window due north; its walls, though, are eighteen inches thick, at least near the base.

Tradition has it that bachelor Mad Jack Fuller used this curious and comfortless place to entertain lady-friends of a class and type that he could not well admit to his residence. But the worthy squire of Brightling Park weighed some twenty stone, and it is questionable whether he could pass through the constricted entrance, whether alone or accompanied by the lady of his current choice. Once inside, perhaps the amenities were more attractive than they appear to be today.

Mad Jack was a man of parts. Stand in the doorway and look north. You will see on the next ridge the obelisk known as the Brightling Needle, and his four-square Observatory, dominating the landscape; also the great wall he had built to relieve current unemployment. He was twice an MP. Offered a peerage, he bluntly refused it: 'I was born Jack Fuller,' he declared, 'and Jack Fuller I'll die.' This gesture was characteristic of a man in whose veins ran good Sussex blood.

14

Freston Tower, Freston, Suffolk, five miles south of Ipswich. Possibly the oldest of our Follies, dating back to about the middle of the sixteenth century. It can be seen better from the estuary of the Orwell than from A138, for the lane to it dips off the road, to end in a field overlooking the river and estuary. It rises six storeys to an ornate parapet and lantern, made all of mellow brick, lavishly windowed on all sides, and with a half-octagonal windowed excrescence running its full height on the estuary face. It cannot be more than about fifteen feet or so square.

Lord Freston built it, with a purpose in mind more specific than just that of gaining a Prospect, charming as that would have been and, indeed, is to this day. In it he incarcerated his daughter, Ellen, whose beauty he was resolved to match with learning. On the ground floor she was to practise the virtues of charity, one day a week; on the first floor, she was to weave intricate tapestry; on the second, study music; on the third, read the ancient tongues; on the fourth, study the work of English writers; on the fifth, study painting; and on the sixth and final floor, observe the stars in their motions and learn wisdom from the astrologers. Presumably the seventh day was for her a day of rest, when she could sunbathe behind the parapets, or perhaps return home for a change of scene and activity. However attractive the view, surely she was to be pitied for being at the mercy of so exacting a father-taskmaster.

The rear view, which confronts you as you cross the field, is the least attractive, but the easiest to photograph; it is not enhanced, however, by the presence of a farmhouse abutting on to it. The best view might be from a boat, using a telephoto lens, for it could then be seen clear of its attendant trees. A compromise is from the south side, when its stiff vertical lines are softened by the branches of oak trees lower on the steep slope beneath it. They would not have been planted when the tower was built, and the view out from the windows (assuming that the poor child ever had time to look out through them) must have been splendid in all directions. It is its commanding presence that has led some to deny the story of Lord Freston and his daughter Ellen, and to say it was built as a look-out river tower.

Egyptian Aviary, Tong, Shropshire, off A41, just north of the village. A few hundred yards up a lane to the west of the Newport-Wolverhampton main road you come to Vauxhall Farm, on your left; at the end of the farm approach, clearly visible from the road, stands this odd edifice, known as the aviary, though in fact designed as an elaborate hen-house by an eccentric named George Durant in the early part of last century. The date inscribed on the stone cap is so weathered that it is difficult to see whether it reads 1812, or 1842; no matter, for the date is less important than the story behind the building, and that of the odd character who designed and built it.

It is shaped as a steep-sided square pyramid on a palish red sandstone base, and rises in four diminishing tiers of coloured encaustic bricks to its capstone twenty feet or so above ground level. In each side are ventilation orifices outlined, like the quoins, in darker brickwork. You may doubt whether, in fact, it was intended as a hen-house; but if not, why the inscription AB OVO on the top? (Or is there some occult implication in the two Latin words?) It is popularly called 'Egyptian' because it is in the style of the pyramids, though much more modest in scale.

There are other inscriptions: 'Live and Let Live', says one; 'Scrat Before You Peck', says another, more relevantly; and a third, vaguely relevant: 'Teach Your Granny'. Do they throw any light on the odd fellow who built this (among several other Follies in the neighbourhood)? His motto, a pun on his name, was *Beati Qui Durant*—Happy are those who Endure. He it was who demolished much of neighbouring Tong Castle, which came into his possession, utilising some of its materials for his various Follies, such as the Pulpit in the wall by the roadside. These 'endure', though he is dead these many years. But his eccentricity is immortalised here; and he is remembered, too, for his generosity in building a cell to house a 'private hermit', one Carolus, who certainly lived more comfortably than a medieval hermit ever did, thanks to the philanthropy of his employer, George Durant, a man, obviously, of a humorous turn of mind, as may be seen by a close examination of the many bits of his Follies in the neighbourhood which still survive the man who created them.

Radway Castle, Edgehill, Warwickshire, seven miles north-west of Banbury. A Sham Castle—or what? It stands on a ridge to the north of the level plain on which, on 23 October 1642, was fought the first battle of the Civil War, the Battle of Edgehill. (At the foot of the hill stands the memorial stone to those who fought and died there.) Allegedly, King Charles I raised his standard on this ridge, above the plain; it was to mark this traditional site that, a century after the battle, an amateur architect named Sanderson Miller, of Radway Grange near by, erected this edifice, known both as Radway Tower/Castle and Edgehill Castle/Tower. He had already experimented in pseudo-Gothic work by building such facades on to various houses on his estate; this, however, was his *chef d'oeuvre*, his vaunted masterpiece.

It is constructed of palish yellow freestone: a massive octagonal tower, originally flanked by two squat, square towers, one of which has now been reduced to a villa-sized dwelling-cum-inn. The tower rises to some seventy feet, spectacularly machicolated and, at the top, corbelled outwards from the main walls, with their narrow, Gothic-type windows. It is easy to imagine defenders in some desperate medieval siege (centuries before it was built) dropping stones and molten lead on to the attackers below. Easy to imagine, too, that there was once a drawbridge and a wide moat at the foot of the tower —though of course the whole thing was built centuries later than the tradition it so deliberately imitated and fostered.

In fact, there was formerly a miniature drawbridge spanning a modest moat; but now greensward spreads about the base of the tower, contrasting pleasantly with the colourful stonework. You can still see the buttresses on which the drawbridge was laid. Inside the 'Castle', now a welcoming inn, you may gaze your fill at specimens of armour and weapons worn and used by the men who fought that far-off battle on a warm October Sunday afternoon. It is a peaceful spot; hard to envisage the sounds of battle percolating through the trees and undergrowth that clothe the slopes of the hillside that rise so steeply to the ridge. Certainly within those solid walls you would be safe even from the ghostly echoes of those battle-cries today.

20

2 WINDMILLS

THE MOST engagingly picturesque examples of construction to be seen any-where in the country are the windmills: they possess a quality of aliveness not to be found in any other buildings (even bridges). They depend for their lives on the wind, and so are associated in the mind with movement—even volition. To see a windmill's sails begin to turn at the bidding of a breath of wind imper-ceptible at ground level is to experience a moment of magic; it is an experience that can never pall.

The earliest form of windmill, the Post Mill, was first known here eight centuries ago. We know this because they appear in contemporary illuminated manuscripts. The oldest surviving Post Mill is the one at Bourn, Cambridge-shire, dated 1636; the one at Outwood, Surrey, dated just thirty years later, runs it very close. It has the merit, not possessed by the other, of being capable of grinding even today: each windy Sunday afternoon it grinds corn for sale to lovers of stone-ground flour.

Though our prevailing wind comes from the south-west, almost all surviving windmills are to be found in eastern counties. There are specimens (additional to those shown in the following pages) at Rottingdean, Halnaker Hill, Chailey, Barham Downs, in Sussex and Kent; at Great Chishill, Mountnessing, West Wratting, Madingley, Bourn, Peasanhall, Syleham, Friston, Thorpeness, in East Anglia; at Wrawby, Legbourne and Skidby, in Lincolnshire and York-shire; at Stevington, Brill, Pitstone Green and Quainton, in Bedfordshire and Buckinghamshire. This, of course, is by no means the whole tally, but represents some of those easily located and well worth photographing.

A century, two-three centuries ago, windmills proliferated. Every suitable ridge, summit or mound (often including prehistoric barrows that offered the advantage of artificial height amid otherwise level ground) would have its windmill—often several, strategically placed so as not to 'take the wind out of each other's sails'. Most have long since disappeared; but often they have left a memory in the form of a place-name such as Windmill Hill, or even a street-name containing the word. And a keen-eyed searcher may sometimes find, in the crown of some mound, the 'cross' left indented by the arms of the support to a long-vanished Post Mill.

The first mills erected consisted of the body, or 'crown-tree', containing the machinery and stones and supporting the 'cap' and the sails (or sweeps), which could be pivoted on the massive central pillar so as to turn the sails 'into the eye of the wind'. Sometimes the supporting cross-frame is visible; sometimes this was enclosed within a 'round-house' built of brick and used as storage-space. In Salvington Mill this has been converted into a ground-floor dwelling.

In the seventeenth century came the Smock (or Frock) Mills. These were larger, constructed of weather-boarding, usually octagonal or even twelve-sided. They were built solid from the ground upwards, the only part of the whole to turn being the 'cap', carrying the sails, and the 'fantail' which was used to turn the cap into the wind's eye. With the much smaller Post Mills the miller could do this by hand, or with a system of cog-wheels, ratchets and chains; it was very hard work.

In the same century came the Tower Mills, taller even than most of the Smock Mills, built of brick in the form of lighthouses, multi-windowed. Though admittedly statuesque, they lack the beauty and 'life' of the weather-boarded Smock Mills, and all too often the brickwork is tarred or painted in heavy black paint.

Tower Mill, Billingford, Norfolk, on A143, four miles east of Diss [previous page]. Probably the finest surviving windmill of the type—and the brickwork has, happily, been left untouched. It was built rather more than a century ago, replacing a much older Post Mill on the same slight mound. It was still in regular use after the Second War War. Some indication of its proportions is given by the Renault Caravelle at its base.

Union Smock Mill, Cranbrook, Kent [opposite]. This is unquestionably the noblest Smock Mill in the country. Built in 1814, it was in constant use until some twenty years ago, and has been maintained in excellent repair by its miller owners, who employed Dutch mill-wrights to fit new sails and other gear not long ago. It stands over seventy feet high, one of the highest in the country, towering above the mean outbuildings at its feet which present problems to the photographer anxious to do it full justice. It dominates the little township, as its predecessors must have done from this site.

Post Mill, Saxstead Green, Suffolk, on A1120, fifteen miles east of Stow-market [top left]. This beautifully preserved specimen dates back to the late eighteenth or possibly early nineteenth century and overlooks a pleasant green alongside a private house whose owners have established on their lawn a scale-model of the mill that towers above their roof. The mill possesses a 'fantail' braced at the foot of the stairs by which it is entered above the round-house. The depth of the feathered weather-boarding can be judged from the shadow-pattern thrown on to it by the sweeps.

Smock Mill, Shipley, Sussex, off B2224, six miles south of Horsham [top right]. This Smock Mill, like the Union Mill at Cranbrook, is octagonal and possesses a gallery corbelled outwards from the base. In a relatively flat and featureless landscape it stands out proudly, visible for miles in almost every direction, giving somehow the fanciful impression that it is a lighthouse rising from a sea of green turf. It is no longer in use, but the owners who live along-side are always willing to show bona fide visitors over their property, for a modest fee; it is well worth while.

Tower Mill, Burnham Overy, Norfolk, on A149, ten miles east of Hunstan-ton [bottom left]. Built about 1816, it is now National Trust property, and incidentally occupied as a private house—obviously by people who take justi-fiable pride in maintaining it in perfect condition. Black-painted, it is true—as are most windmills of this type; but the windows, door and spacious gallery as well as the cap and sails are picked out in brilliant white to afford a satisfying contrast. At the foot of its hill slope is the attractive Burnham Overy Watermill, dated 1795.

Tower Mill, Pakenham, Suffolk, off A143, four miles north-east of Bury St Edmunds [bottom right]. Built about 1810, it is one of a small handful of such mills that still fulfil the purpose for which they were built; it is the only survivor in its class in Suffolk. When this photograph was taken (unhappily on a dull day), experts were at work checking the sweeps for signs of deterioration; others were checking the wear on the gearing of the giant wind-shaft and the toothed head-wheel, ten feet in diameter and subjected to enormous strains as the huge sails keep it in motion.

3 LOCK-UPS

THE LOCK-UP is a traditional eighteenth century feature of the English village. Into it the common malefactor was thrown to cool his heels until he could be brought before the magistrate for sentence. It ordinarily stood on the village green (as at Harrold and Kingsbury Episcopi); or adjacent to the village pond (as at Shenley) in which the local scolds were ducked; or it might be incorporated with the nearest bridge (as at Baslow); or again (as at Deeping St James) it would be sited close to the church.

The majority of lock-ups are round. Even if they are octagonal or square they are still locally called Round-houses. Other names for them are Pounds, Pin-folds, Lob's Pounds, Cages, and Blind Houses. The last name is apt since they are ventilated solely by small, heavily-barred grilles above eye-level that offer the luckless occupant the minimum of light and air. The walls, often two feet thick, rise to about head height and carry a domed or conical stone roof, sometimes (as at Castle Cary and Shrewton) topped by a neat finial. A low-lintelled, narrow oak door is heavily studded with square-cut nails (the Heytesbury lock-up has two hundred and fifty of these). There may be an inner door (as at Shenley), or an iron grille through which the prisoner may be observed without risk. Through it he may also receive his bread and water.

The Castle Cary lock-up, Somerset, on the A371 Shepton Mallet road [top left], was built in 1779 for £23, 'provided by local charities'. Unusually, it has three stone steps, up which the prisoner would be roughly thrust, ducking his head to avoid injury.

The Kingsbury Episcopi lock-up, Somerset, three miles north of South Petherton [top right], is octagonal, with a particularly fine jointed-stone conical roof and finial, an unusually narrow doorway, and a pair of grilles vertically placed and narrow to match.

The Shenley lock-up, Hertfordshire, two miles east of Radlett [bottom right], is earlier than most, being seventeenth century. Unusually, it is white-plastered over, resembling an iced cake; it has a Gothic-arched doorway and door to fit. Two inscribed panels dated 1810 offer advice to the prisoner and those gloating over his fate well worth pondering: *Do Well* and *Fear Not. Be Sober* and *Be Vigilant.* Admirable if ironic advice!

The Shrewton lock-up, Wiltshire, six miles west of Amesbury [previous page, bottom left], stands beside the bridge at the western exit to the village. Massive domed roof and walls appear to have been built in one piece of the forbidding grey local stone, softened by lichen.

The Lingfield lock-up, Surrey, four miles north of East Grinstead [top left], is dated 1763. It stands near the pond, half-engulfed in an enormous oak tree struck by lightning so that its hollow trunk is now the playground of small children. Tradition has it that this was an Act of God precipitated by a particularly foul-mouthed individual incarcerated in what is locally called the Old Cage. In a niche there once stood St Peter's Cross; but it vanished when lightning struck, leaving the prisoner stunned, dazed, but unrepentant; indeed swearing, they will tell you, harder than ever.

The Baslow lock-up, Derbyshire, four miles east of Bakewell [top right], is incorporated in the fourteenth century bridge over the Wye. Square, with a heavy slab roof, its severe lines are redeemed by the presence of two oval port-holes set, for once, at prisoner's eye-level, so that he could gaze hungrily at the freedom he had had snatched from him.

The Harrold lock-up, Bedfordshire, eight miles north-west of Bedford [bottom left], stands at the end of an avenue of limes spanning the village green. It possesses an unusually fine conical roof of graduated stone laid in undulating courses. In a massive staple you may see the original giant padlock, of which the constable held the only key.

The Deeping St James lock-up, Lincolnshire, nine miles east of Stamford [bottom right], is more ornate than most. Two tiers of stone seats surround the square walls, terraced inwards to a squat spire now topped by a lamp. The stone walls are lined with brick, from which three niches have been hewn to contain the prisoners squeezed into them and manacled by heavy chains, still in position. Almost completely lacking in ventilation, and with a 'capacity audience', it must have been a miniature Black Hole of Calcutta.

There are plenty of other lock-ups to be located and photographed; the Pinfold at Breedon-on-the-Hill, Leicestershire, with its graceful weather-vane, for instance. A particularly fine one existed till recently at Heytesbury, Wiltshire: octagonal and built into a stone wall lining the main street. It was unhappily demolished by accident, but is to be rebuilt, its finial replaced, thanks to the Lord of the Manor.

4 PREHISTORIC

ENGLAND IS extraordinarily rich in prehistoric remains. Though you may perhaps feel that archaeology is not for you, it is in fact a subject that can exercise a quite remarkable fascination, and can well become a lifetime hobby. Once know what to look out for, and you will find examples on every hand, one leading persuasively on to the next as you move about the country. The Ministry of Works, the National Trust and other official bodies have been diligent in taking steps for the preservation of such features of the countryside, though there are innumerable specimens that have not as yet come within their jurisdiction or received their paternal blessing.

For the enthusiast there exist maps of Prehistoric Britain; and there are countless books on every aspect of the subject. The first may well serve as a springboard; the second will answer in detail all your questions. The choice is limitless: Long and Round Barrows; Dolmens, Menhirs, Cromlechs, Quoits; Standing Stones, Stone Circles, Hut Circles, Iron-Age Forts, Earthworks, Lake Villages, Cairns, Tombs, Henges, Flint Mines; Monoliths, Megaliths, Passage Graves, Burial Sites; Sarsens, Cists, Celtic Crosses, Ogham Stones; Celtic Fields, Cursus, Arrow Stones, Grey Wethers, Inscribed Stones, Strip Lynchets and Causeways—you name them, we have them!

For the photographer, the subjects vary greatly in photogenic quality. Long and Round Barrows and turf-covered features generally are difficult to photograph effectively, for they tend to flatten-out into the landscape as a whole, however well they have been sited by the men who laboriously constructed them, perhaps four or five thousand years ago. But very often the earth has fallen away, or been removed by men searching for alleged buried treasure, and all that remains will be the massive stone framework that originally protected the burial from being crushed by the sheer weight of earth and stone superimposed upon it. Then the photographer comes into his own: these great stones possess a dignity innate within their sheer mass that responds well to the camera lens. There are innumerable examples of these, up and down the country: in Cornwall and the West Country generally; in Wessex; in the Severn Valley region; and also far to the north; and far to the east, in Kent.

Trethevy Quoit, Trema Coombe, Cornwall, three miles west of Liskeard [previous page]. To locate this fine specimen of a Burial Tomb entrance, from which all the earth and turf have long since been removed, take a minor road (B3254) for a short distance and then an even smaller road through a small hamlet and onwards up a steep hill between close-set banks. At the top, the lane opens out and, on your left, close at hand but dominating the skyline, towers this magnificent specimen. A plaque informs you that it is of the 'Early to Middle Bronze Age, 1800-1200 BC' and that it is 'of a type unusual in East Cornwall'. The stone, of course, is the local Cornish granite: a type of stone that lasts for ever and shows hardly any sign of the weathering that character-ises the softer oolitic and even the carboniferous limestones.

Less than a mile from this Dolmen (here known as a Quoit, and in Wales generally known as a Cromlech) may be found the Stone Circle shown on the map as The Hurlers, or Minions, along with an ancient stone inscribed to King Doniert, who flourished hereabouts in the ninth century AD. And many miles to the west, on a minor road (B3312), four miles north-west of Penzance, is the famous Lanyon Quoit, older by a good deal than Trethevy: 'One of the Penwith Group of Gallery Graves, a Southern Irish form, neolithic, possibly as early as 2,000 BC.' It is much more easily located.

Devil's Arrows, Boroughbridge, Yorkshire, off A1, just outside the town [opposite]. Standing Stones are among the most spectacular examples of pre-historic remains; they have stimulated curiosity throughout the centuries and assembled about themselves a wealth of names, and the inevitable legends too. Probably the finest group in all England, these neolithic monoliths stand, two in a field and one alongside a house on the opposite side of the road, in full view of the Motorway that bypasses Boroughbridge to the west of the town. It is believed that there were formerly five in all; only three survive today, the largest of them twenty-two feet in height. They stand in an almost straight line, about a hundred yards apart from one another. In addition to their great height and girth, and the impression of splendid isolation they impart, their chief feature is the array of grooves, or scars, that run from top to bottom.

34

These have aroused speculation in many generations of sightseers, for the stone of which these monoliths are composed is North Country millstone grit: hard, rough in texture, resistant. So, are these grooves simply the result of weathering? Or are they—as many experts hold—the work of the men who erected them here four thousand years ago? Is there some meaning in their varying depth, their relationship one with another? Or are they, as has been held by other experts, the results of generations of weapon-sharpening? The last suggestion is the most picturesque; but what sword-wielder was tall enough to utilise the upper part of a twenty-foot high stone? Was there, once, a race of giants? Do their graves lie below? We enter, by such speculation, the realm of fancy and fairy-tale. Still, it is these deep vertical incisions that give character to the sheer mass of gritstone in every case. Shown on the previous page are four photographs of only three individual stones; you may like to speculate as to which stone has been photographed twice—and why.

Grooved Monolith, Duddo, Northumberland, six miles north-east of Cold-stream [opposite]. This is not, in fact, a free-standing stone, like the Devil's Arrows, but one of a number forming the Duddo Stone Circle, but presented here in close-up because its grooving is so strikingly emphatic. Once again speculation exists as to whether this is natural grooving, the result of thirty or forty centuries of weathering on this bleak Northumbrian hill top, or the result of sword-sharpening in the Middle Ages when Border warfare was at its height. It can hardly be proved, one way or the other, but the first seems the likelier explanation. Whichever is the answer, however, the carving on this shapely monolith merits the closest scrutiny; it varies with the time of day; you might take a score of photographs in close-up, and obtain a different 'portrait' with every exposure. There are countless other such stones dotted about the country, some larger, some smaller; none of them surpass this in character. The low-angle shot, when you are fortunate enough to have a 'photographer's sky', is the one that will leave you with the most memorable impression. You might even feel that it is a clenched fist rising menacingly out of the rough turf.

36

Arthur's Stone, Dorstone, Herefordshire, off B4348, ten miles west of Hereford [top left]. This fanciful name has been given to a collapsed neolithic tomb of the 'Severn-Cotswold type used for collective burial about 2000 BC'. It is noteworthy rather for its fine situation than for its state of preservation. From this hill top you have a magnificent view across the appropriately named Golden Valley, that lies on the east side of the range of hills grandiosely known as the Black Mountains.

Flint Mine, Grimes Graves, Norfolk, off A134, five miles north-west of Thetford [top right and bottom left]. Flint is found in and beneath chalk; it was used for the earliest tools, and weapons, by neolithic man, at least five thousand years ago. The finest known flint mine is in a field just off the main road, close to the village of Brandon, where, to this day, flint-knapping is still carried on by one family that has been in the business for generations. The 'mine' is some thirty feet deep: a series of pits of varying depth, intercommunicating where the 'black flint', the finest quality, is found. You can see flame marks from the fat-burning lamps used by the earliest miners; you can see also specimens of fossilised antler-picks discovered in these pits, used by the neolithic miners to break out the flints from the chalk; and you can see the chippings they left behind them when they had taken the best for their own use.

Inscribed Stone, Roughtinglinn, Northumberland, six miles north of Wooler [bottom right]. There are not many such inscribed stones in England. This magnificent specimen is on a hill slope in a remote corner of this northernmost county, some six miles to the south-east of Duddo Stone Circle and Pele; it is well worth the search. But you will be puzzled by the series of target-like concentric circles, a foot and more in diameter, skilfully inscribed in the face of this vast tilted slab of rock. The pattern is sometimes known as 'Cup-and-Ring', and each may be linked by a straight or wavy line to its neighbour. They are almost certainly Bronze Age in origin, though this cannot be definitely proved. Similar inscribed slabs in Spain have been held to be symbolic of the Earth Mother, or Earth Goddess. Study them long enough, and you can evolve any number of other theories—none of which can be proved true or false.

5 ROMAN REMAINS

The Roman Wall, Northumberland. Commissioned by the Emperor Hadrian and begun by the Roman Governor of Northern Britain, Platorius Nepos, in AD 122, this is the noblest surviving relic of Rome's occupation of Britain, and one of the finest Roman relics anywhere in Europe. It was designed as a frontier work, a line of demarcation, spanning northern England from Wallsend-on-Tyne in the east to Solway Firth in the west, a distance overall of more than seventy miles, though in fact it was never extended to its full length. The greater part of the completed portion is sited on the Great Whin Sill, an escarpment of whinstone that crosses Northumberland, facing north over the moors that extend the whole way to the Scottish Border. Behind the Wall runs the great east-west road known as Stanegate, linking Newcastle with Carlisle. The Wall, therefore, is easily accessible for almost the whole of its length by offshoots of this road; sometimes without even leaving the road, which in parts lies almost beneath the foundations of the Wall itself. It offers magnificent walking.

The Wall varied in width and height when first constructed some eighteen centuries ago; it varies still. But there are many stretches of several miles in length on which two can walk abreast, six or eight feet above ground level, following the sinuosities, the undulations, of this astonishing landmark mile after mile without let or hindrance. Some of the best stretches are, as here, eastwards from Haltwhistle Burn over Melkridge Common and Steelrigg at 1,000 feet above sea-level and on towards Hotbank Crags high above the gun-metal waters of Crag, Greenlee and Broomlee Loughs, with the great fort of Housesteads dominating the whole. Or you can walk westwards from this same point by way of Great Chesters and the Nine Nicks of Thirlwall to Gilsland and Birdoswald: there is not much to choose between the two stretches of the Wall, but perhaps that to the eastwards, and Housesteads, is the more splendid of the two.

Whichever way you walk, however, it is to the north of the Wall that the ground drops sheer: the Romans knew a thing or two about utilising the lie of the land for their roads and fortifications generally; though the Wall was built not so much as a fortification as a line of demarcation.

Pharos, Dover Castle, Kent. Though the exact spot where the Romans landed in England is still debated (many believe that it was Walmer Beach, six miles north-east of Dover), there is no doubt that very early in their occupation of England they constructed a lighthouse on the high cliff-promontory to the east of Dover (Dubrae, as they called it). This remarkable structure dates from somewhere towards the end of the first century AD. Their word for it is pharos; the French word is *phare*.

It had stood on its rounded green hill for something like a thousand years before Dover Castle was built; many centuries, even, before the earliest of the Saxon fortifications that ringed the hill, antedating the present castle. In spite of its formidable age it has weathered well, at least on the landward side, though Channel gales have wrought havoc with the masonry on the seaward side. Originally it was probably eight storeys in height: this is an assumption based on the immense thickness of the lower stages of the walls. At that time the parapet surrounding the uppermost storey would have been some eighty feet above ground level, though this has long vanished and the structure is considerably less high than it used to be. It is octagonal at base, the massive walls enclosing a chamber some fourteen feet across. As the flint-rubble walls, cased in ashlar and Roman-brick bonded, rose, they were stepped-in about a foot at each storey, so that the diameter steadily diminished with its growing height. There were openings on several sides, notably facing south and east, and the original Roman entrance arch may be plainly seen, but entered only at your peril.

In the Middle Ages new work was constructed above the four lowest Roman stages, and some of this medieval masonry can still be seen; the uppermost stage carries a shield generally attributed to Sir Richard de Pembridge, Constable of the Tower in 1369. When the Saxon Church of St Mary in Castro was built alongside, the Pharos was 'adopted' to serve as its west tower, though it is detached from the main fabric, in which some of the Roman Pharos material has been incorporated by the thrifty Saxon builders. Today the Pharos stands lightless, staring out through empty eye-sockets across the Dover Strait by which, two thousand years or so ago, its builders arrived.

Mosaics, Chedworth Villa, Gloucestershire, off A40 Cheltenham-Northleach road [top right and left]. This second century AD Roman Villa is not actually in Chedworth but approached via Yanworth, well signposted thereafter. 'Villa' in this context is not what we usually mean: it is a wealthy Roman's country house and estate, including, often, a farm. There are several such in England, notably Bignor in Sussex, and Lullingstone in Kent. Chedworth was 'discovered' by a gamekeeper digging out a rabbit-warren. Examples of the tessellated floors he laid bare, shown here, were a characteristic feature of such villas, a type of status-symbol, if you will. You will also be interested in . . .

Hypocaust, Chedworth Villa [bottom right]. This was a standard feature of all well-appointed villas and also of staging-posts such as that at Wall (Roman Letocetum), Staffordshire, on Watling Street. A paved floor was laid over the 'mushrooms' set at intervals so that heat from a wood-fired furnace could circulate freely among them, warming the room above. They were set wide enough for small boys to crawl among them, removing the ash. It was a form of central heating which we have copied in our electric underfloor heating of today. The Romans were civilised when we were no more than savages!

Outer Golden Pot, Chew Green, Northumberland [bottom left]. The Roman Dere Street runs intermittently northwards from High Rochester to the Scottish Border at Coquet Head, Cheviot, passing through an isolated camp shown on the map as Ad Fines (the Roman, perhaps, for 'The Utter Limit'!). Two massive stone bases are shown in microscopic type on a large-scale map of the area: bases, probably, for ancient boundary stones. They are named Outer and Middle Golden Pot; and they offer a challenge to the determined walker who can map-read, use a compass, and who, wisely, carries also a whistle for emergency, for sudden changes of weather can swiftly blot out the surrounding countryside. Here, perhaps, is the last refuge of truly wild scenery, awesome in its solitude. There are few marks of latter day civilisation, and you may well feel that the Roman colonists shared the exact same view—truly living history.

6 MEDIEVAL

THE TERM is used here loosely. The selection that immediately follows is wide in its range, and may well be challenged by purist and specialist. No matter: our aim is to stimulate curiosity rather than, specifically, to inform; a host of books by experts will answer the serious questioner who seeks academic information.

Church Porch, Kilpeck, Herefordshire, off A465 Hereford-Abergavenny road, seven miles south-west of Hereford. This may take some finding; but your effort is generously rewarded. The Parish Church of Saints Mary & David, at Kilpeck St Devereux (a mile south-east of the main road, over the railway line), is acknowledged by experts to be one of the finest existing specimens of a smallish Norman church. It dates from the year 1134, though on this site there was almost certainly a much more ancient church dating from Saxon times, a fragment of which may still be detected by anyone prepared to examine thoroughly the buttress on the north-west side of the chancel.

The chief glory of the church, however, is the superbly proportioned and carved doorway, formerly protected by a porch that is no longer to be seen but must have contributed to its preservation throughout its eight centuries of existence. It is an elaborately ornate doorway, sculptured in great detail and, clearly, by a most gifted artist-craftsman. The doorway jambs represent Eden, the Temptation and the Fall of Man after the eating of the fatal fruit of the Tree of Knowledge of Good and Evil. Examine it intently, and you will see that the Serpent has been carved with its head downwards—symbolic of the belief that Evil must eventually know defeat.

There is more symbolic carving in the panel between the square lintel and the Norman arch above it: here Creation is portrayed, with a fine array of birds, beasts and fishes, among other figures. The magic about this doorway (apart from the miracle of its conception and its preservation) is that each time you return to study it you will discover more entrancing details that you had previously overlooked. The church hopes to raise sufficient money to add a new porch, in keeping with the style of the whole, to replace the vanished one, and so ensure that the rare beauty of the doorway will be preserved during the centuries yet to come.

Chantry on Bridge, Wakefield, Yorkshire. Edmund of Langley founded this most beautiful Chantry about 1350 AD, eight years after toll-rights had been granted to the bridge on which it stands. Of the four surviving Bridge Chapels (the others are at St Ives, Huntingdonshire, Rotherham, and Bradford-on-Avon, Wiltshire) this one is incomparably the finest. It is in the Decorated style at its most profuse, especially externally. Its facade is composed of five bays and three narrow, pointed doorways in them. Above the five pointed arches are five rectangular panels beneath a castellated parapet containing finely carved reliefs of the Annunciation, the Nativity, the Coronation of the Virgin Mary, the Resurrection, and the Ascension. There is a wealth of decorative tracery and the whole is topped by beautifully proportioned crocketed finials. The sides have three windows apiece and a wealth, again, of flowing tracery, including graceful cinquefoils and five-petalled flowers.

In the north-east corner there is a stair-turret to a low-pitched roof; to the right of the east window there is a niche designed to contain a statue; below part of the Chantry there is a crypt-like sacristy connected to the chapel itself by the spiral staircase in the north-east turret. There is fine carving in the interior, too.

The Chantry has had a chequered history. It has been an old-clothes shop, a library, a corn-factor's office, a cheesecake shop. It was long ago found in need of drastic restoration, and this was carried out in the last century, when the original facade was transferred to Kettlethorpe Hall, in the hope that it would survive better there, while the new facade, faithfully copying the original, was carried out in a stone that might resist the weather more successfully, though this can hardly be guaranteed, for its site is well in the Yorkshire industrial belt.

Its chequered history ended in the mid-nineteenth century, since when it has been regularly used for its original purpose (other than the collection of bridge-tolls, for which it used to serve), namely for worship. Services are held there frequently, and baptisms too; though probably not weddings or funerals. The scrollwork on the doors is singularl beautiful, and the nine-arched bridge well worth detailed study.

Pele (or Peel) Towers are found exclusively in the far north of the country, close to the Scottish Border on either side, and date from the fourteenth century. They were stoutly fortified dwellings, built to resist onslaught: immensely thick walls contain two, three or four rooms, one immediately above the other, in which womenfolk and children were relatively safe, while their lord (or laird) did battle with the aggressor below. Very few of them, after six centuries, are better than impressive ruins.

Duddo Pele, six miles north-east of Coldstream, Northumberland [top left], is typical in its decayed massiveness, but characterised by the remains of what must have been an exceptionally well designed corbelled turret on one corner, just discernible today.

Elsdon Pele, four miles east of Otterburn [bottom left]. An unusually massive pele tower incorporated in later building and thus better preserved than most. It was for many years the 'fortified vicarage' of the incumbent of the ancient Church of St Cuthbert, the only one known in the country. It dominates the green, and the church below it.

Doddington Pele, three miles north of Wooler, Northumberland [bottom right], shows clearly the look-out and arrow-slits and retains part at least of its original gable. But it has become incorporated in farm outbuildings, a great deal of its stone removed from it to make byres and cart sheds and the like: the fate of ancient splendour at the mercy of grasping man. Corrugated-iron roofing insults its fine facade.

Priory Gateway, Dunwich, Suffolk, on the coast, three miles south of Southwold [top right]. Little remains today of the thirteenth century Priory save a few yards of flint wall here and there, and a ruined flint arch now the entrance to farmland; little remains, either, of the 'City of Dunwich', a legendary 'lost city' of palaces and cathedrals and stately edifices, swallowed up by the remorseless seas that have been eroding the cliffs of East Anglia for untold centuries. Today, they will tell you locally, you can hear the church bells ringing out, fathoms deep beneath the treacherous sea. Debussy might have written his *La Cathédrale Engloutie* of Dunwich (or of Crantock, Cornwall) though he not unnaturally chose a legendary site in Brittany instead. This is a place that haunts, though so great a part of it has vanished beneath the waves.

50

The dove-cote has been a feature of the countryside ever since medieval times; they were known earlier than that on the other side of the English Channel; and the Romans made use of them centuries earlier still. They were not designed to gratify the owner with Tennyson's 'Moan of doves in immemorial elms' but for a purely utilitarian purpose, a twofold one at that: to supply the owner's family with meat when beef and lamb and pork were scarce; and to provide additional fertiliser for his pastures. Like lock-ups, they may be round, square, octagonal, gabled or domed. They rarely possess beauty; but they form part of a simple, traditional, satisfying economy.

Chastleton, Oxfordshire, off A44, two miles west of Chipping Norton [top left]. Opposite the early seventeenth-century Chastleton House, it is more ornate than the medieval cotes: four gables, the whole built on massive pillars, and topped by a lantern.

Belleau, Lincolnshire, off A16, about eight miles south-east of Louth [top right]. Octagonal, red brick, slate-roofed, it stands in Belleau Manor Farm and, oddly, is known locally as the Guard House. The innumerable niches inside reveal its true function.

Garway, Herefordshire, off B4521, seven miles north-west of Monmouth [bottom right]. Perhaps the noblest round dove-cote of all. It was built by the Knights Templar in 1326 AD. Its circular wall is four feet thick, the interior diameter seventeen feet. Inset in the wall are six hundred and sixty-six pigeon-holes, tier upon tier to the lantern by which the birds enter, six inches square, eighteen inches in depth, with an alighting-sill projecting from each successive tier. It stands close to the twelfth-century Church of St Michael, one of six attributed to the Order of the Knights Templar.

Willington, Bedfordshire, four miles east of Bedford [bottom left]. Undoubtedly the giant of them all! Rectangular, with stepped roof, it is entered by either of two low doors, each admitting you to a separate, square chamber rising to a cathedral-like height. Each chamber contains sixteen tiers of nesting-sites, complete with ledges, ten to a tier; the total capacity, therefore, is almost double that of Garway: twelve hundred in all. It is less ancient, however, than that built by the Knights Templar: sixteenth century only. But it rides the flat landscape like some fine cathedral.

52

Well-Chapel, Dupath, Cornwall, off A388, two miles south-east of Callington [top left]. The best-preserved of Cornwall's well-chapels, built in the sixteenth century to serve as a baptistry and preserve the holy well beneath its massive roof of moorstone. The site (as so often) was probably a pagan one, sanctified in medieval times by the Christian Church as the new Faith spread further into this 'outlandish' corner of the country. Inevitably it has an accretion of legend. Local belief is that it was built as a penance by a Cornishman who had slain a rival for the hand of the woman he loved.

Parson's Dove-cote, Collingbourne Ducis, Wiltshire, two miles north-west of Ludgershall [top right]. Look closely at the handsome church tower of St Andrews and you will spot a square opening with sill below. What is it? Until about 1500 AD the incumbent used the tower as his private dove-cote; then bells were installed and he had to give it up. Thirty-two foot-high curved steps set in an extremely narrow spiral stairway lead you past the opening to the belfry, surrounded by three hundred nesting-sites, long vacated by their occupants, even by their ghosts, thanks to the jangling bells.

Teazle Tower, Woodchester, Gloucestershire, three miles south of Stroud [bottom left]. Close by the main road, in a field that slopes down to it from the heights above, stands this attractive cone-capped stone tower, with Gothic-arched doorway and scattered small windows. A building near by was formerly a woollen mill. In this tower were stored the teazles required for use in processing the wool from the flocks of sheep that gave this neighbourhood its wealth and reputation for so many centuries.

Hermit's Cell, Roche Rock, Cornwall, five miles north of St Austell [bottom right]. In a landscape dominated by china clay tips, the granite mass known as Roche Rocks catches the eye, growing out of a near-level field. And 'growing out' of its summit is a man-made hermitage of hewn granite blocks. It is a fourteenth-century chapel-cum-cell dedicated to St Michael. Legend has it that a hermit, struck down by leprosy, incarcerated himself here, to spare his fellows. His daughter, St Gundred, devotedly brought water to him daily from a well near by. From the top of the ruined chapel a magnificent view may be obtained for miles in every direction over the strange landscape.

7 MARKET CROSSES AND CROSS SHAFTS

ONE BY one during the Middle Ages and later, small towns and larger villages acquired the right to hold markets at which buyers and sellers from a wide area of which the place would be the centre did business weekly or monthly. A focal point for such business was of course necessary, and to begin with this might be a simple shaft on a pedestal as near as possible to the centre and in some open space where people could forgather. As a hint that honesty in dealing must be maintained, the shaft would be surmounted by a cross. Often the handiest place for the newly named Market Cross would be near the church, further emphasising the need for fair dealing between vendor and purchaser. In time, say by the end of the fifteenth century, the Market Cross, the shaft, with tiers of stone steps surrounding it which could be used for displaying wares, and for sitting on, was elaborated. This was as much as anything to offer comfort to those doing business there and so to promote better salesmanship. The shaft would be roofed over, beneath the cross, and an arched wall be built round it—square, hexagonal or octagonal. Such market crosses are frequently objects not only of historic interest but of great architectural and sculptural beauty. They dominated the local scene for centuries, eventually to be replaced by the covered markets of many towns today. Some of them, of course, unhappily fell victims to road-widening schemes and other examples of modern progress, and so we know them only from contemporary engravings today. Unquestionably, the two finest surviving examples of the Market Cross at its best are those at Chichester, Sussex, and Malmesbury, Wiltshire; but there are many others only just less impressive in various market towns.

Market Cross, Chichester, Sussex. By common consent this is the finest in the whole country, though the one at Malmesbury runs it fairly close. It was the gift to the city, by a Deed of 1501, from Edward Story, Bishop of Chichester 1478-1503. It stands in the heart of the city, at the junction of North, South, East and West Streets, streets that follow the compass points as laid out by Cissa, the Roman who founded the city and gave it his name. The Cross stands fifty feet high, a graceful and elaborate structure built in stone from Caen, across the English Channel.

It is an open-arcaded octagon with a massive central column supporting a lierne vault with carved bosses at the intersections of the ribs. Beneath each Gothic arch is a carved bishop's mitre, and above each are twelve cinquefoiled panels. Above these is a frieze of rosettes, animals, foliage and other figures, and above these again a succession of beautiful crocketed finials. The angle buttresses support most satisfyingly proportioned flying buttresses, delicately crocketed, which merge into an ornate crown, which itself carries a lantern and a cross.

Over the long centuries the Market Cross has inevitably suffered, and undergone a succession of changes. Here, the clock faces are relatively modern, replacing the ones originally presented to the city by Lady Farington in 1724. As a tribute to her public-spiritedness, the arms of her family have been added to those of Henry VII, in whose reign the Cross was erected, those of Bishop Story, the munificent donor, and those of the city itself. Formerly the bishop had his own bust in a niche facing down East Street, but this was replaced by a seventeenth-century bust of Charles I, and the bishop's bust was relegated to the Cathedral where he was appropriately buried. Most of the niches, that originally contained statues, are now sadly empty: evidence both of vandalism and iconoclasm down the centuries. For all that, however, in its proportions and symmetry, in its sheer imagination of design and perfection of execution, this Market Cross, four centuries and a half old, remains the crown of them all.

Market Cross, Malmesbury, Wiltshire [opposite]. This is the only Market Cross which can begin to sustain comparison with that at Chichester. Though it cannot claim quite such perfection of design, at least so far as its main fabric is concerned (the lantern, certainly, outshines that of its West Sussex rival), it is built of a stone that is warmer, more beautiful in hue and texture, than the Caen stone of the other. It is some nine feet shorter than the Cross at Chichester. It, too, is octagonal but its arches are lower, wider, perhaps clumsier, less decorated, than the others, and the fact that stone benches now fill in the bases of several of them detracts a little from their symmetry. The architraves above them are castellated.

The buttresses, which carry a good deal of ornamentation in their upper portions, sustain flying buttresses which curve gracefully to support, at their point of union, the handsome and lofty lantern that begins at the level of the crocketed finials capping the main buttresses. The lantern is lavishly ornamented with small, close-crowded statues of the saints and scenes from the Crucifixion. Above them is an even more elaborate carved crown, and this in turn supports a lofty and exquisitely proportioned finial rising to rather more than forty feet from the ground. It was of this noble market cross that the sixteenth-century antiquarian John Leland wrote: 'A right fair and costely peace of worke in the market place made al of stone and curiusly voultid for poore market folkes to stande dry when rayne cummith upon them.'

Butter Cross, Oakham, Rutland [top left]. This simple but shapely Cross stands isolated in a small square overlooked by the buildings of Oakham School. It is octagonal, with a steeply pitched roof of fine Collyweston slates supported on eight massive square oak posts. Round a central stone column supporting the apex of the roof there are tiers of stone seats. Embedded in the cobbled floor there is a set of medieval oak stocks. Take a second look and you will notice a curious feature: the number of holes in the stocks is odd, not even. Does this mean that one habitual occupant was one-legged? There is another example of the stock-maker's apparent inability to count, in the porch of the tiny church of St Feock, near Truro, Cornwall.

Wool Hall, Pembridge, Herefordshire, on A44, six miles west of Leominster [top right]. This late fifteenth-century structure is unusual in that it is rectangular. It consists of a heavy stone-slabbed roof supported on eight massive pillars of squared oak set in the steeply sloping surface of a triangle of ground immediately opposite the very ancient 'New Inn'. This inn was for long known as 'The Inn Without a Name'; for a time it served as the Court House for the whole district, and in it, according to tradition, the Treaty ending the Wars of the Roses was signed. This was a wool centre—hence the name of the Market Cross, where dealers and purchasers used to meet. One of the oak pillars is based on a stone plinth known as 'The Preacher's Stone'.

Itinerant priests in the Middle Ages and later used to call here on market days and harangue those present, whether they had come to buy or sell or stare.

Market Cross, Shepton Mallet, Somerset, on A37 Bristol-Yeovil road [previous page, bottom left]. This small market town bestrides the main road that runs almost due south from Bristol. The road widens temporarily at a junction with a side road where this hexagonal structure stands: the place has manifestly been a gathering-ground throughout the history of the town. The Cross dates from about 1500 AD. Though it has no flying buttresses, it has a most attractive carved frieze running round the top of the six arches and carrying crockets and pinnacles that are matched by those on the tall and slender shaft that soars from the centre. The shaft contains niches now sadly denuded of the statues for which they were originally designed. Over the entrance that faces southwards down the main street there is a pleasing specimen of a working sundial.

Market Cross, North Walsham, Norfolk, ten miles south-east of Cromer [previous page, bottom right]. This one bears an inscription: 'Built in 1549 by Bishop Redman; Re-built in 1600 by Bishop Redman after a Great Fire; Restored in 1807 by the Town's Worthies.' It is octagonal and consists of eight oak columns supporting an elaborate three-tiered roof topped by a clock in a turret and a weather-vane where the true cross once stood. A brick plinth supports the posts, evening-out the road sloping down through the present market place, where an open-air market is still regularly held, having long overflowed the restricted area of the market cross. The floor is of round pebbles embedded in cement.

In the centre stands the well preserved ancient fire-engine belonging to the town: a manually-operated wooden contraption with heavy handles for four men to work in pairs opposite one another. Immediately overhead is an elaborate ceiling-skeleton of massive oak beams interlocking with one another at subtle angles. Not surprisingly, this market cross is scheduled as a National Monument.

Market Cross, Stalbridge, Dorset eight miles south of Wincanton [opposite]. This one was never enclosed. It is a tall, slender cross shaft carved in mellow-toned local stone, with small figures carved on its face, all softened in outline by the weathering of its six centuries of existence. The uppermost section has been restored.

62

Yarn Market, Dunster, Somerset [top]. It is known also as Butter Cross. This fine medieval Market Cross stands at the top end of the broad main street that climbs from the foot of Dunster Castle to the beautiful Luttrell Arms Inn. Its octagonal plinth of russet stone carries a broad sill of iron-hard oak between each of the massive oak pillars supporting the wide-spreading slate roof, a roof in two pitches interspersed with gabled dormer windows fitted with diamond-leaded panes. The upper pitch of the roof rises to a lantern, which is the finial of a massive cylindrical stone central column.

Poultry Cross, Salisbury, Wiltshire [bottom left]. The city formerly possessed four Market Crosses: Cheese Cross, at the south end of Castle Street; Wool Cross, in New Canal; Barnewell's Cross, in St Barnard's Street; and Poultry Cross, at the end of Butcher Row. The last-named is the sole survivor. Hexagonal in plan, it is characterised by four-centred arches with blank ogee-tips and stepped buttresses. Above the ogee-tip of each arch there is a graceful canopied niche that formerly contained a statue. Each is separated from its neighbour by well proportioned stone rails. Slender flying buttresses spring from the main buttresses, to meet and support an elegant lantern, topped by a cross. A succession of crocketed pinnacles add grace to the whole. Unhappily, this Cross stands close to a road along which traffic surges ruthlessly past within a foot or two of the nearest buttress: any day now could be its last, and this most attractive Cross would vanish into the limbo with its old companions.

Butter Cross, Witney, Oxfordshire [bottom right]. This Market Cross is less ancient than many others, dating only from the seventeenth century. Four steeply-pitched gables with herringbone panelling and ornamental barge-boards rise above a tiled roof supported on a succession of stone pillars and capitals. Witney has long been famous for the manufacture of blankets, from the wool of the famous Cotswold flocks of sheep; but beneath this roof, traditionally, butter was sold, and to this day you will find market stalls displaying variegated goods beneath that gabled overhanging roof.

64

8 NATURAL FEATURES

IT WOULD have been easy to fill this book, and a hundred of similar length, without going outside this category. Sarsen stones, Hanging woods, Fossils, Scarps and Scars and Caves, Swallet-holes, Waterfalls, Logan stones, 'Shivering' mountains, Cliffs and Edges and Becks and Scree: the list is limitless, endlessly varied; the problem is where to start and end. So—a mere handful, to whet the appetite for search.

The Devil's Chimney, Leckhampton, Gloucestershire, three miles south of Cheltenham [top left]. This is a natural stack of oolitic limestone, weather-eroded down the centuries. It stands proud on the western scarp of the Cotswolds, reminiscent, on a minor scale, of Orkney's Old Man of Hoy. To reach it, take the Birdlip road (B4070) and branch off at the sign to Salterley Grange Hospital. A goat-track climbs steeply from a quarry opposite the hospital gates, levelling out after a strenuous mile. From this scarp you have a superb view westwards across the Severn Valley to the Forest of Dean and Wales, and north-westwards to the Malvern Hills. Do not attempt to climb the stack (though it has been done by experts), for the stone is treacherous, and if you are betrayed it means a fall of many hundred feet to the valley road far below.

Clints, Malham Cove, Yorkshire, five miles north of A65 Settle to Skipton road [remaining photographs on this page]. This is the local name for these formations in the carboniferous limestone that preponderates in this region of the Pennines. Limestone plateaux have been water-worn by thousands of years of rain, snow and frost into these fantastically beautiful patterns; in the natural seams, or 'grykes', in the stone, Nature, like some skilled stone-mason, has been endlessly at work with natural mallet and chisel. Feel the stone, and it will strike you as iron hard; it is immeasurably harder than the Cotswold stone of the Devil's Chimney. But it is easily water-worn, and is merely repeating on the surface what has been going on deep down below for aeons to produce the pot-holes, caverns and passages beloved of the dedicated speleologist. Botanists will find these clints happy hunting-grounds for rare and beautiful flora.

The Major Oak, Nottinghamshire, off B6034, half a mile north of Edwin-stowe [see next page]. A five-minute walk through Sherwood Forest leads you to this extraordinary survivor.

It is the largest, if not the tallest, tree in the country. It is a Samson among oaks, forty to fifty feet in girth at breast height, half as much again at ground level, its lower boughs as massive as many an oak-tree bole. A dozen and more people can be accommodated at once within its lightning-blasted shell. It is claimed to be at least six centuries old; certainly it exudes an aura of antiquity that seems to date it back well beyond the age of the baronial castle and the pele towers of the Border.

Yew Garden, Packwood House, Warwickshire, on B4439, two miles south-east of Hockley Heath [top right]. These are the outliers of the extraordinary 'Sermon on the Mount' garden planted here by one John Fetherston around 1660. The main garden contains a host of yews, including twelve enormous ones known as 'The Apostles' and four similar ones known as 'The Evangelists'. A box-lined aisle leads to the noblest of them all, appropriately named 'The Master', or 'The Pinnacle of the Temple'.

Lulworth Cove, Dorset, on coast, ten miles east of Weymouth [bottom left]. Here you may witness the effect of the sea's action on strata that have been extravagantly distorted in remote geological periods. Horizontal bedding-planes have been violently up-ended, twisted, spiralled, contorted, and then attacked by the aggressive waves and their burden. The resultant shaping of what you might think to be wholly resistant rock is clear evidence of the enormous power of the elemental forces that have been at work subterraneously over the ages. This can be paralleled in many parts of our coastline, notably at Gull Rock, Wellcome, North Devon, and the appropriately named Whale Rock, Bude, North Cornwall.

Durdle Door, Dorset, on coast, ten miles east of Weymouth [bottom right]. Here is a 'stack' in the making. A section of the Portland stone of which these cliffs are partly made has been worn through by the incessant battering of the waves and the loose stone they carry. In due course the 'roof' will cave in and the outward portion be left free-standing, a new companion for the stacks rising from the water along this Purbeck coast. More spectacular examples may be seen all round our coastline, particularly off the north-east coast, as at Flamborough, and further north too, off Caithness.

68

9 BUILDINGS

WHERE TO start and stop, what to include, omit? Churches and cathedrals, inns and tithe-barns, alms-houses, priories and priests' houses: the choice is infinite. The few examples that follow could have been multiplied several hundredfold; every individual could have been replaced by half a hundred deserving alternatives; and there would still have remained an inexhaustible supply, interesting and photogenic enough.

Kirtling Gate House, Cambridgeshire, four miles south-east of Newmarket. This splendid mellow red-brick, stone-quoined edifice stands just south of the ancient flint-and-stone Church of St Philip. Velvet lawns make a smooth carpet for its feet; clipped yews, unextravagant topiary work, shelter beneath it; two smaller octagonal towers merge with the house screened behind, just visible to left and to right of it. It dates from the mid-fifteenth century, the reign of Henry VI. Princess Elizabeth, afterwards Queen Elizabeth I, was a state prisoner here, under the charge of Edward, first Lord North, who became MP for Cambridgeshire. He was Chancellor of Henry VIII's Court of Augmentation, responsible for dealing with the confiscated monastic properties and other great estates. His official duties enabled him to enrich himself enormously—at the expense of the many whose properties he handled to his own great advantage. So, he lived here in great style for many years: a man of power and position. We do not know what his residence looked like in his day, though ordinarily the mansion would range symmetrically to left and to right of the Gate House (as at Oxburgh, Norfolk, not many miles away, with its magnificent Gate House and moat).

Unhappily, many years after North's decease, his mansion fell into ruins. Today, virtually all that remains of the original structure is the Gate House itself, which would certainly have been its noblest (and most substantially built) feature. Stand well back from it, and consider its symmetry and, as it were, massive gracefulness: the proportions of brick to stone, of mullioned window to brick and stone, of height to breadth and depth. The fine central bay windows thrust out boldly and beautifully between the flanking octagonal towers and above the noble doorway; the diamond-paned windows in the two towers give a hint of secrecy: a princess was incarcerated here.

Minack Theatre, Porthcurno, Cornwall, three miles from Land's End. You may be inclined to protest that this hardly qualifies as a 'building'. Well, perhaps not; for there is precious little construction-work in evidence. Nevertheless, it deserves inclusion—if only on the grounds that it is unique in its *genre.* Incidentally, it takes some finding. Follow either the main A30 Penzance-Land's End road, branching off on to B3283 for St Buryan, Treen and Porthcurno; or B3315 Penzance-Land's End minor road and watch out for signs labelled 'Minack Theatre'.

This unique open-air theatre is the brain-child of Rowena Cade. Nearly forty years ago she began work, virtually single-handed, to adapt a suitable portion of this granite cliff-face, two or three miles short of Land's End itself, almost sheer beneath her house, to serve as a theatre in the ancient Greek tradition. The raw material of her 'building' was the granite of the cliff. Her first task was to level sufficient of the cliff above the sea to constitute a stage as understood by Euripides, Sophocles and Aeschylus. As the stone was hewn out and removed it was transformed into tiers of stone seats, in the same tradition. Green Rooms for the actors were fashioned out of coigns in the cliff-face, interspersed among the granite columns left standing. The theatre, wide open to the sky above, and to the crawling sea far beneath—the junction of the English Channel with the vast Atlantic to the west—is what a dedicated visionary 'saw', four decades and more ago, and wrought out of virgin rock with her own hands, and those of a small band of devoted helpers. A dream slowly became a reality: a theatre was born in the unlikeliest of settings. And what a range of performances has been seen in this unlikely setting! T. S. Eliot's *Murder in the Cathedral;* Racine's *Phaedra;* Anouilh's *Ring Round the Moon;* Bernstein's *West Side Story; The Murder of Maria Marten;* Behan's *The Hostage; The Merchant of Venice, Measure for Measure* and *Twelfth Night;* Marlowe's *Dr Faustus;* Bolt's *A Man for All Seasons;* to mention a handful only. The performances have been given by a wide variety of Repertory and other Companies, such as the Leicester Drama Society, Oxford's Trinity Players, the West Cornwall Theatre Club and the Comedy Club of London.

House-in-the-Clouds, Thorpeness, Suffolk, three miles north of Aldeburgh, along the coast road, B1353. This extraordinary building—a freak of fancy, certainly, and equally certainly not to everyone's taste—is to be found just west of the hamlet of Thorpeness, on the edge of the sandy, bracken-strewn levels from which a small golf-course has been made. It rises from a little copse of silver-birch and shrub, five storeys high, of brown weather-boarding, with stepped windows on each floor artistically picked out in white—much as is done with the windows in windmills that have been adapted to private occupation. At every window are curtains: proof that this is indeed a house. But —look again. The part of the structure that really resembles a house is perched on top of the weather-boarded support, and there are no curtains at those windows. Why? Because in fact this uppermost part of the whole structure, in dull red weather-boarding by contrast, and roofed with matching tiles, is no house at all but the water-tank that produces the head of mains water for the villagers whose houses and cottages are scattered about its feet! Proof that this is so is to be found in the fact that the tell-tale 'mouse' used to indicate the level of water in the tank beneath that roof, and behind the dummy windows, may be descried high up beneath the eaves, if you look closely enough.

It is not, of course, old; let alone ancient. In fact, it was constructed in between the two World Wars. An old man in the village recalls having worked on it, but will not be persuaded to say what, really, he thinks of this local freak. But he emphasises that, freak or not, the House-in-the-Clouds (the name, at least, has a touch of child-poetry) is popular; especially with overseas visitors. It is privately owned, for letting to holiday-makers (especially those with children, who adore living there) in this corner of East Anglia. Immediately opposite the building you will find one of Suffolk's best-preserved Post Mills, privately owned, too, and maintained in excellent repair. The photograph was taken from behind it, through one of the sweeps. Behind this you can descry the chimney-pots. If by some unlucky chance this House-in-the-Clouds caught fire, at least there would be water at hand!

74

We may think of buildings in terms of the regions in which they are found: the granite of Cornwall, slate of Lakeland, golden limestone of the Cotswolds, harsher gritstone of the Pennines, heavy half-timbering in Cheshire and down the Welsh Border; or we may think simply of periods: Jacobean, Queen Anne, Georgian, Victorian, and so forth. Less obvious an approach, perhaps, is that rewarded by the locating of the primitive in building-method. For example: Cruck-building. This dates back into the Middle Ages, tentatively survived a century or two, and was the prerogative of the cottager.

The Cruck consists of a curved oak trunk that has been split down the middle and the matching halves then erected so as to unite at the top and straddle the base. A second pair was then erected at a suitable distance and linked to the first by a ridge-pole. That was the bare skeleton; it was then filled in with brick-work, wattle-and-daub or other rough material, sometimes supplemented by cross-beams and verticals. Few examples survive today. Odd ones may be tracked down near the Welsh Border, in the West Midlands, in Gloucester-shire, Shropshire, Warwickshire, even in Wiltshire and Berkshire; chiefly where there has always been a supply of good standing timber. They represent the survival of the earliest known form of above-ground building.

The Barley Mow, Long Wittenham, Berkshire, three miles east of Abingdon [top left]. Jerome K. Jerome's Three Men in a Boat tied up here, for the inn stands alongside the Thames dividing Berkshire from Oxfordshire. Snug thatch embraces the points of the crucks.

Cruck-ended cottage, Maxstoke, Warwickshire, seven miles north-west of Coventry [top right]. These are unusually slender and gracefully carved crucks, with only one strengthening cross-beam, near the top, bestriding three well-matched diamond-paned windows.

Cruck-ended cottage, Lacock, Wiltshire, four miles south of Chippenham [bottom left]. Only half the cruck now shows, the matching member having been absorbed into an adjacent building, more's the pity; a modest feature of this National Trust Priory village.

Cruck-ended cottage, Putley, Herefordshire, eight miles east of Hereford [bottom right]. A 'blind' cruck-end, windowless, on a plinth of brick and sub-stantially braced with tie-beams between which, to its advantage surely, a window or two might have been inset?

76

Moot Hall, Aldeburgh, Suffolk [top left]. The 'Little Parliament' of Aldeburgh still meets in this miniature building on the sea shore, four centuries old; its fine sundial carries the words: *Horas Non Numero Nisi Serenas*. Twin chimneys dominate the brick, stone and oak edifice, entered by a fine staircase on the landward side. Among its treasures it houses a painting of a group of nineteen villagers, all identified. Near by is the slipway down which the village sent the *Marygold*, with a picked local crew, to fight the Spaniards under Sir Francis Drake.

Church, Lullington, Sussex, five miles north of Seaford [top right]. Fifteen feet square, it challenges Culbone, Porlock, as the smallest-in-England. It seats eighteen, close-crowded, and has font, lectern and altar contained within massive flint walls broken by slender lancet windows and topped by a tiled roof and squat weather-board belfry capped by a broach spire. It is probably the chancel of a larger church, the foundations of which lie half-buried in the turf to the west. A track across these fine Downs will lead you, in a couple of miles, to the Long Man of Wilmington.

Bell Tower, Brookland, Kent, six miles north-east of Rye [bottom left]. Reminiscent of a Norwegian *stavkirke*, this massive bell-turret stands detached from the corner of the Church of St Augustine, on Romney Marsh. Its eighteen-inch-square main timbers form a pointed arch strong enough to take the weight of the peal of five bells installed in the sixteenth century, though the church itself is much earlier than that. The oak was floated down the Rother from the Kentish Weald; not (as is traditionally maintained) salvaged from a ship wrecked off the coast in the fifteenth century.

Saxon Church, Greenstead-juxta-Ongar, Essex, ten miles west of Chelmsford [bottom right]. A Shrine of St Emund, King of the East Saxons, martyred by the Danes in 870 AD, and 'the oldest wooden church in the world' (though the Norwegians would challenge this). Its nave is unique in that it is made of split tree-trunks set thin-edge-to-edge, tongued and grooved. It dates from 845 AD, when it was built on a site where pre-Christian Celts had worshipped amid the trees of ancient Hainault Forest: the name Greenstead means 'a clearing among the trees'. It is older than its attendant yews.

10 MEMORIALS

MEMORIALS UP and down the country are legion: war memorials; memorials to battles fought; to kings and queens; politicians and philanthropists; soldiers, sailors and airmen; writers, preachers, composers—the list is endless. Many are unworthy in design, thoughtlessly sited; others catch the eye, fire the imagination, arouse curiosity. All mean, or have meant at some time or other, something to somebody.

Dover Patrol Memorial, St Margaret's-at-Cliffe, Kent, off A258 Dover to Deal road. Few memorials are more splendidly or appropriately sited than this one. A short lane leads out of the village, to end on the cliff top. Towering from its massive plinth into the Kentish sky is a huge, tapering obelisk of stone, square cut, pyramidally capped. It commemorates the gallantry of that heroic body of men who saved Britain from starvation and surrender in the First World War: The Dover Patrol.

A panel inset in the east face of the plinth bears the words: 'To the Glory of God and in Everlasting Remembrance of the Dover Patrol, 1914-1919. To the Memory of the Officers and Men of the Royal Navy and the Merchant Navy Who Gave Their Lives in Ships Sailing Upon the Waters of the Dover Strait.' A panel inset in the north face of the plinth bears the words: 'The Monument to the Dover Patrol Was Erected by Public Subscription Together With Those at Cap Gris Nez, France, and New York Harbour, America.' They are simple words, all the more memorable for their straightforwardness.

An oak seat stands against each face of the plinth, overlooking the well-kept turf that so effectively sets off the cold grey stone soaring above it. At each corner of the turf surround there stands a massive anchor, symbol both of the vessels that sailed beneath these cliffs and of the hope they inspired in those who remained at home. A stone's-throw distant is a small, octagonal coast-guard station, on the very edge of the cliff. Through its powerful swivelling binoculars you can on a clear day watch the traffic on the French mainland twenty-two miles away. Apart from the steady stream of vessels rounding the cliffs and dodging the treacherous waters of the Goodwin Sands, five miles off shore, this is the only traffic the coastguard ever sees during his lonely stints of duty 257.9 feet above the English Channel.

80

Grace Darling Memorial, Bamburgh, Northumberland [top left]. It was placed at the highest point of St Aidan's Churchyard so as to be visible from the sea; her actual tomb is nearer the church. One stormy night in 1838, when the Bamburgh boatmen refused to launch their boats, this twenty-three-year-old girl persuaded her father, Keeper of the Longstone lighthouse, to row out with her to the ship *Forfarshire*, shipwrecked off the great cliffs. They rescued nine survivors and tended them at the lighthouse. Four years later, Grace Darling died of consumption. The small cottage in which she was born faces the churchyard; next door is a small, intimate Memorial Museum which contains the rowing-boat and many of the girl's simple, personal possessions.

Waggoners Memorial, Sledmere, Yorks, seven miles north-west of Great Driffield [top right]. Erected by Lt- Col. Sir Mark Sykes, the local squire, 'As a Remembrance of the Gallant Services Rendered by the Waggoners' Reserve, a Corps of 1,000 Drivers Raised on the Yorkshire Wold Farms in 1912'. Ornate bas-reliefs depict English heroism in battle, 'Hun' brutality, civilian devotion, waggoners on Flanders roads, Sir Mark himself.

Eleanor Cross, Geddington, Northants, three miles north-east of Kettering [bottom right]. Only three of the original eleven memorial crosses erected by Queen Eleanor's funeral cortege between Hardby, Lincolnshire, and Westminster Abbey survive today (the third is at Waltham, Essex). The niches of this slender and intricately carved shaft contain three statues of the queen, beneath gabled canopies, carved in 1294. They are fortunate to have survived the old village sport of squirrel-stoning: squirrels were placed on the masonry and stoned as they leapt frenziedly about in terror, seeking desperately to escape the missiles.

Eleanor Cross, Hardingstone, Northants, on A50, one mile south of Northampton [bottom left]. The earliest one, carved in 1291 by John Battle. Above the stepped base the arcaded pedestal carries the shields of Ponthieu, Castille, Leon and England. Above it, three niches enshrine statues of the queen, of whom her sorrowing husband said: 'Living, I dearly cherished her; dead, I shall not cease to love her.' Above, there is a square, elaborately carved pillar designed to carry the cross, whose shaft is now truncated.

82

The Percy Stone, Otterburn, Northumberland, one mile west of Otterburn [top left]. This small, shapely obelisk commemorates the Battle of Otterburn fought here, as a plaque duly records, on 10 August, 1388. It is named after the legendary Percies of this fierce Border country. Smaller than most such memorial stones, it has a simple, poignant dignity not dwarfed by the vast sweep of moorland that reaches to the Cheviots behind it, or the Northumbrian moors stretching southwards right to Hadrian's Wall.

Flodden Field Monument, Branxton, Northumberland, off A697, four miles south-east of Coldstream [top right]. This most impressive monument stands on a low mound overlooking the saucer-like plain on which the English, on 9 September ('Black Friday' to the Scots) defeated and slew James IV of Scotland and 10,000 of his fighting-men, in a battle immortalised by Sir Walter Scott in *Marmion*. The memorial was erected in 1910. Annually, in the early part of August, there is a cavalcade of a hundred horsemen to the site; a wreath is laid on the cairn which supports the granite cross, and a memorial service is held, with an address which, by tradition, pays tribute to the valour of the soldiers of both sides who died in the battle 450 years ago.

Edgehill Memorial, Radway, Warwickshire, off B4086, seven miles north-west of Banbury [bottom left]. Half a mile from the village, approaching the steep rise to Edge Hill, stands a stone by the roadside some five feet high, round as a barrel. It records that 'Between Here and the Village the Battle of Edgehill, the First of the Civil War, Was Fought on Sunday, 23rd October, 1642. Many of Those Who Lost Their Lives in the Battle Are Buried Three-quarters of a Mile to the South of This Stone.'

Cyclists Memorial, Meriden, Warwickshire, off A45 Coventry-Birmingham road [bottom right]. This stark granite obelisk was erected 'In Remembrance of Those CYCLISTS Who Gave Their Lives in World War II, 1939-1945'. So, it is not a memorial to cycle-borne dispatch-riders of an earlier war but to the countless thousands of cycling enthusiasts who died in the various armed forces. Appropriately enough, the memorial stands on a village green reputedly in the dead centre of England; a region, incidentally, that has always been noted for the activities of cyclists and motor-cyclists.

11 BRIDGES

First, the shallow ford; then the natural, or man-placed, stepping-stones; then the tree-trunk thrown across water too deep for either; then the more permanent stone slab (the Clam-bridge); then the succession of slabs, on stone piles, linking bank with more distant bank (the Clapper-bridge); then the timber-built bridge, replaced by the stone-built bridge, packhorse or vehicle-carrying. And so to the cantilever and suspension bridges of today, in high-tensile steel. It is an engrossing story, one that can be literally illustrated by wandering round the country, camera in hand.

There are more bridges in England of all these, and other, types than would be within any one man's competence to count. They range from the primitive clam to the graceful perfection of the new Severn Suspension Bridge; they carry buildings or an oratory; they are fortified; they are clapper; they are packhorse; they are 'freak' bridges; but the list is endless. You could well spend half a lifetime in search of the ancient, the medieval, the historic, the exceptional, the beautiful, the strange and the extravagant; and at the end of that time be just beginning to recognise the hard fact that you had but touched on the fringe of a theme that is alluring, compulsive—and inexhaustible.

Whatever its type, a bridge can rarely fail to be essentially an object of beauty, representing the perfect balance of the functional and the aesthetically satisfying. That rare specimen, the clam, will convey the strong impression of being exactly right for the purpose for which it was laid: a single slab of stone linking the banks of a narrow stream too deep to ford and liable to flow so strongly that it would wash away anything lighter than stone. The clapper (its first development), linking the banks of a wider stream also liable to flood: this offers the pleasure of observing well-matched slabs skilfully laid on stone pedestals stout enough to bear their immense weight and firmly enough embedded to resist, with their top-structure, the full impact of water in spate, swollen by winter rains and melting snow on the hills. If the surrounding terrain is low-lying, subject to flood, there will often be a stone causeway at each approach, to carry the traveller or pack-train across it.

You may well wonder why, with plenty of stone in evidence, clapper and clam bridges never have parapets. The reason is not far to seek: a vertical parapet would either cause the water to bank up above the bridge, or be broken down by its sheer weight. Better that the swollen water should wash smoothly over it till the spate subsides.

For obvious reasons, none of the really early timber-built bridges survive today. But the medieval stone bridges that replaced them exist in their many hundreds, if not thousands: small and large, simple and ornate, multi-arched or single-span, narrow and wide. In flat country, with water-meadows (as at Shardlow, Derbyshire), they may be remarkable for their great length, the sheer number of their consecutive arches; in hilly country they may be more spectacular, loftily spanning gorges in which there may be a sudden rise of many feet in water level, almost without warning. The thirteenth-century Devil's Bridge at Kirkby Lonsdale, Westmorland, is an excellent specimen. It is probably true to say that in no other type of bridge is there such variety to be found, or such a richness of architectural inspiration and masons' skill. Often enough it is the small bridge, the lowly single-arched packhorse bridge such as that at Beckfoot, a few miles to the north of Kirkby Lonsdale's Devil's Bridge, or the one at Ovingham, near Hadrian's Wall, that will be remembered longer even than some of the more ambitious stone bridges much easier to pinpoint on the map and well signposted.

Like windmills (but for the diametrically opposite reason) bridges, even the smallest ones, are relatively easy to locate. They will be found, of course, where water runs (or used to run), and this will naturally be at the lowest point in the landscape. Where the road dips; where, in dry terrain there is a hint of clustered trees; where a hamlet nestles almost out of sight from the slopes above: there, almost certainly, is the object of your search, awaiting discovery. It may or may not bear a name; it may have a hostelry alongside, named Bridge Inn; it may have a signpost to warn you that it is unsuitable for heavy traffic; it may be catalogued among historic monuments, officially protected by the Ministry of Works; but it will be there! It may (like the bridge at Eynsford, Kent) bestride the stream with the old ford alongside.

Pulteney Bridge, Bath, Somerset [page 87]. This is the nearest approach we have in England to Florence's incomparable Ponte Vecchio. It was designed by Robert Adam, under the patronage of Sir William Pulteney, in 1769. Its three semicircular arches span the Avon as it flows leisurely through the centre of the city and over a diagonally-set weir on the downstream side. A carriageway nearly thirty feet wide runs between what were, in its heyday, gracefully designed two-storey private dwellings, though now they have been largely replaced by small lock-up shops. This comes nearer to the tradition of the Florentine bridge, with its twin rows of jewellers' and goldsmiths' boutiques; nearer, therefore, to the medieval London Bridge with its crowded tenement houses and cramped shops and booths. But Robert Adam, for all his genius, must be taken to task on one count: the buildings are set solid along both sides of his bridge; at no point (save from some window if you happen to live there) is it possible to look out along the stretch of bright water that runs so smoothly over the weir; a man on a bridge should always be able to watch the water flowing beneath it.

High Bridge, Lincoln [previous page]. There was a bridge here, across the Witham, in the heart of the city, in Norman times: a massive ribbed arch ten feet high and twice that in width. What you see today, however, is a later bridge constructed over the same arch and carrying a four-storey half-timbered building, much of which dates from the mid-sixteenth century. Unlike Pulteney Bridge, the building, which today includes a restaurant, stands on one side of the bridge only; a narrow flight of stone steps on either side leads down from the road to the towpaths alongside the river. It is very narrow here, squeezed between the springing of the arch. The barge you see had rammed it, and become locked solid. It took two tugboats in addition to its own engine, to free it, after several hours. The barge operator at the tiller may or may not have reflected with satisfaction that the traditional name for the arch he was attempting to shoot is—the 'Glory Hole'. Heavy traffic in High Street beyond is, so far as is practicable, diverted, to spare this medieval bridge and sixteenth century top-structure from the inevitable and potentially disastrous wear-and-tear.

Oratory Bridge, Bradford-on-Avon, Wiltshire [previous page]. This is a late thirteenth or very early fourteenth-century bridge of nine stone arches spanning the Avon on the south side of the little town. Two of the arches are original; the seven others date from the sixteenth century. At the southern end there is a most charming small oratory corbelled outwards and upwards from one of the piers. It dates back some three centuries and has been used (to the authorities' shame) not only as an oratory and shrine to St Nicholas, whose emblem, the gudgeon, is commemorated in the graceful copper weathervane that tops the edifice, but also as a powder magazine and, for even longer, as a lock-up. Among those who have been incarcerated within its cramped confines is the preacher, John Wesley, who spent an uncomfortable and undeserved night there in 1757. That it served as a lock-up led to the local saying that a man might spend his days and nights there 'under the fish and over the water'. Incidentally, the name of the town comes from the fact that, long before the bridge was built, a ford lay beneath the water: it was a Broad Ford—Bradford-on-Avon.

Fortified Bridge, Monmouth [opposite]. This bridge (originally much narrower than it is today) was built across the River Monnow as long ago as 1272, and is thus almost exactly seven hundred years old. It was soon widened, to carry horse-drawn traffic into and out of 'Welsh Wales', and was fortified from the start to protect the town from incursions from beyond 'Wales-in-England' (this is, so to speak, a hybrid county). The arch is original, but when the bridge was widened, the flanking towers were thrown up and the archway encompassed and so strengthened. Look carefully, and you can see above the arch, immediately over the roadway, projecting masonry from which molten lead and boiling oil and other handy missiles could be conveniently hurled at the attackers as they came within immediate range after forcing their way across the bridge. There used to be a similar bridge defence-tower at Shrewsbury, further to the north along the Welsh Marches, but this has long since disappeared. But an examples survives, on a less impressive scale, at Warkworth, in Northumberland; there the medieval bridge spans the River Coquet just before it spills into the sea.

Clapper, Postbridge, Devonshire, seven miles south-west of Moretonhampstead [top]. The West Country is rich in this type of bridge; this is one of the finest specimens. It dates back at least to the thirteenth century, and may be many centuries older still—even prehistoric. It spans the River Dart close to the Moretonhampstead-Princetown road, within five miles of the infamous Dartmoor prison. Granite slabs up to fifteen feet long and four feet and more wide lie across a succession of massive piers and abutments, approached by steps at each end, the distant approach being marked by a series of granite posts erected to guide travellers in snow and mist. It gives an extraordinary impression of antiquity and concentrated 'memory' of men and pack-trains travelling through the centuries. Not far away is the clapper at Wallabrook, smaller but still impressive; and the famous Dartmeet clapper-bridge, so often spoiled-to-view by the crowds gathered to clamber about on the stepping-stones alongside. There is also the bridge at Teign Head, near Fernworthy. Of the two, the first is the more interesting, since it is hardly more, in fact, than a clam.

Trinity Bridge, Crowland, Lincolnshire, eight miles north-east of Peterborough [bottom]. Its unofficial name is the 'Three-Ways-to-Nowhere' Bridge, and the reason is not far to seek. It stands high-and-dry in the heart of the village, though in the fourteenth century, when it was almost certainly built (and probably by the monks of neighbouring Crowland Abbey, to symbolise, with its three intersecting arches, 'The Trinity'), it spanned three streams: the Catwater, Welland and Nene. There is a local superstition that a bottomless pit containing a whirlpool lies beneath the intersection of the arches, and you may be induced by some local wag to put your ear to the ground to listen to it. The superstition was on record at least three centuries ago, when the bridge was already three hundred years old. You will find on one of its parapets, sadly weathered, it is true, and almost obliterated by the passage of time, the remains of what seems to be a seated figure. No one knows for certain whom it represents, but it could well be the effigy of the patron saint of bridges; or it might be an early Abbot from Crowland Abbey, or some other dignitary of this fenland region.

94

12 ODDMENTS

YOU WILL come across them unexpectedly, often in the least promising districts: relics of the past, the remote past too. They may evoke wonder; they may strike you as macabre; they may amuse, puzzle, arouse curiosity, provoke thought and conjecture. They are well worth seeking out. The examples that follow are but a tithe of the host to be located the length and breadth of the country, from Kent to Northumberland.

Offham is a sequestered Kentish village set in a region of orchards, on the edge of the hop gardens, two miles from the junction of A20 London-Maidstone road and A228 Tonbridge-Rochester road, near West Malling. It possesses a triangular village green overlooked by a variety of houses and cottages. They are built of local ragstone, of red brick and tile-hung; a notable eighteenth-century brick and tile house dominates the green, fronting another of brick, tile, weather-boarding and half-timberering. The old smithy, now tastefully converted into a private house, with a wrought-iron name-plate presenting the old smith at his anvil, and an anvil in the garden, is closest to the green's unique feature, a **Quintain** [opposite]; there is no other in all England.

This medieval device had a twofold purpose: it developed nimbleness and skill in the horse-borne military man; and it afforded entertainment for the onlookers—entertainment tinged with the pleasurable anticipation of danger. An inscription reads: 'The pastime—originally a Roman exercise—was for the youth on horseback to run at it as fast as possible and hit the broad part in his career with much force. He that by chance hit it not at all was treated with loud peals of derision; he who hit it made the best use of his swiftness lest he should have a sound blow on the neck from the bag of sand which instantly swung round from the other end. The great design of this sport was to try the agility of both horse and man, and to break the board; which, whoever did, he was accounted the Chief of the Day's Sport.'

Tilting, in fact: the 'target' being the sixty-dot domino at one end of the swinging arm. The old sport is revived annually on May Day. But nowadays the contestants are pretty girls, and the penalty for slowness or clumsiness is a sudden douche of cold water tipped from a bucket suspended from the arm from which once the sandbag hung.

Steng Cross Gibbett, on B6342, eight miles east of Otterburn, Northumberland. It stands high on a mound beside the road that cuts through Forestry Commission plantations, its arm, eighteen feet above ground level, pointing across the moors to the Cheviots far to the north. It is a thousand feet above sea level, surrounded by Tosson Hill, Simonside, Hindhope Law and Ottercops Moss: grim country, a grim setting for a windswept gallows from which many a common malefactor has dangled and rotted before the eyes of the pack-train men and their convoys passing east and west below his feet. Caught in the neighbourhood in grey weather, you may well fancy you can hear ghosts of those who have died there in days gone past sighing and moaning on the wind.

The gibbet has caught the fancy of writers down the years. One has told its grim story well: 'The gibbet rears its gaunt outline on the hill known as Steng Cross. Strangely enough, this gallows has no connection with the Border raiders, many of whom met their death 'high on the gallows-tree' (as the Border Ballads have it). The present gibbet stands on the site of one from which the body of William Winter was suspended in chains after he had been hanged at the West Gate, Newcastle. Today this grisly relic is called Winter's Gibbet. Winter was hanged in 1791 for the murder of an old woman named Margaret Crozier. According to an old *Guide to Northumberland*, believing her to be rich, one William Winter, a desperate character but recently returned from transportation, at the instigation and with the assistance of two female *faws* (vendors of crockery and tinwork) named Jane and Eleanor Clark, who in their wanderings had experienced the kindness of Margaret Crozier, broke into the lonely pele on the night of 29 August, 1791, and cruelly murdered the poor old woman, loading the ass they had brought with them with her goods. The day before, they had rested and dined in a sheepfold on Whiskershield Common, which overlooked the pele where she lived. It was from a description given of them by a shepherd boy, who had seen them and taken particular notice of the nails in Winter's shoes, and also the particular *gully*, or butcher's knife, with which he divided the food, that brought them to justice.' No news, however, of Jane and Eleanor Clark's fate.

Stocks, Ripley, Yorkshire, three miles north of Harrogate [top left]. They stand in a small cobbled square overlooked by the ancient Church of All Saints (with its unique Weeping, or Kneeling Cross). This set of stocks is so placed that the occupants could sit on the lowest tier of steps forming the plinth of the Market Cross: a refinement they may or may not have appreciated as they sat there at the mercy of all who cared to emphasise their personal freedom at the expense of themselves.

Gibbet, Caxton, Cambridgeshire, on A14 Huntingdon-Royston main road [top right]. This ancient gibbet, admittedly less impressive than the one at Steng Cross, is one of a small handful still to be found up and down the country —though street-names remind us that they were once to be seen at every turn: London's Gallows Corner, and Tyburn Way, at Marble Arch, are such examples. This one stands alongside a main road to the North, much frequented in the eighteenth century by highwaymen; from it, doubtless, many a highwayman has swung. Today it looks down on passing motor traffic, a tacit reminder that to fail to slow down at the roundabout near by could mean death.

Stocks, Little Budworth, Cheshire, off A54, five miles west of Middlewich [bottom left]. This charming hamlet lies on the edge of the 'wich', or 'salt' towns of Cheshire: Nantwich, Northwich and Middlewich. It is a long time since they were in use, but these stocks are among the best preserved still *in situ:* solid oak planks, set in oak slides, bolstered to left and right by massive stone pillars and backed by a wall built of the local russet sandstone that gives warmth and character to the place.

Pillory, Coleshill, Warwickshire, eight miles east of Birmingham [bottom right]. In some respects the pillory was an even more uncomfortable form of punishment than the stocks, often placed near by. For though the prisoner's feet might be free, he was gripped by the wrists (and sometimes the head also), and so could not protect his face from the rotten eggs and other missiles traditionally hurled at him by the mischievous bystanders. This specimen, one of the very few to survive outside the local museums, is attached to a wall on Church Hill, in the centre of the township. Ironically, a notice on one side reads: Members Only; and on the other side: Travel Agent.

Sundial, Seaton Ross, Yorkshire, six miles west of Market Weighton [top left]. On the front of one old cottage in this sleepy little village a twelve-foot-diameter sundial marks the leisurely passing hours. It was constructed by an enthusiast, one William Watson, who made another for the local Church of St Edmund, and a third for his own farm. He died aged 73, in 1857, having written his own epitaph, to be read on his tombstone: 'At this church I so often / With pleasure did call, That I made a sundial / Upon the church wall.' Not far from his grave is that of Margaret Harper, reputedly a witch, who died somewhat earlier. She also wrote her own epitaph, making it clear that she strongly resented the imputation: 'The faults you've seen in me / Strive to avoid; Search your own hearts / And you'll be WELL EMPLOYED.' She wrote with real feeling.

Church Key, Eyke, Suffolk, on B1069, ten miles north-east of Ipswich [top right]. The name of this diminutive hamlet used to be locally spelt I K E. A locksmith cut the wards to represent three letters: I K E. Today, the key he fashioned so skilfully hangs against the wall, a pleasing example of wrought-ironwork in its own right. By pure chance, the three letters, re-arranged, spell the word 'key' in primitive form.

Steelyard, Soham, Cambridgeshire, eight miles north-west of Newmarket [bottom left]. One of only two in the country (the other is at Woodbridge, Suffolk), this is mounted high up on the rear of the Fountain Inn, opposite St Andrew's Church. In olden times it was used to weigh the wagon and its load of corn, slung from two massive chains; it could carry a load totalling two tons deadweight and was in constant use for years.

Inn Door, Batheaston, Somerset, three miles east of Bath [bottom right]. This 1,000-gallon barrel was locally made. It has been inset in the wall of the George and Dragon inn so that half of it protrudes outwards, the other half into the bar. It thus serves as a 'revolving', and draught-excluding door. Not many years ago many owners of licenced premises brewed their own beer, storing it in barrels like this. Duty paid, then, on such a barrel was only— sixpence; today it would be at least £20, or eight hundred times as much! It is easy to miss as you sweep by westwards on A4, making for the beautiful city of Bath. Slow down, though: it is worth more than a passing glance.

Petrifying Well, Knaresborough, Yorkshire [top left]. Water flows over a limestone mass to fall into a natural pool below. A century and more ago a number of oddments such as hats, caps, shoes, gloves, were hung on a line beneath the dripping water. The lime in it has petrified—literally 'turned to stone'—these objects. Visitors today leave oddments such as children's toys, socks, scarves and so forth, to be naturally treated by the iron, lime, magnesia and sulphur; returning after some months, they see the early stages of a process that will be complete in perhaps a year or less.

Signpost, Wroxton, Oxfordshire, on A422 Banbury-Stratford road [top right]. This ancient signpost is known as the 'Carved Hands' post. Carved in relief on the four faces of the weathered stone pillar are life-size hands pointing severally to Stratford, Chipping Norton, Banbury and London; they curve about the post in the most lifelike fashion. Local tradition says the old road to London passed by at its feet. An inscription carved on it reads: 'First Given by Mr White in the Year 1686'. The oak tree in the background was planted to commemorate the coronation of Queen Victoria.

Thames Head, Gloucestershire, off A433 road, three miles south-west of Cirencester [bottom left]. Take a track below the Thames Head inn, crossing a disused railway siding, and follow the path across the field for half a mile. It brings you to the official source of the River Thames. In wet weather you can seen the spring; in dry weather a mere heap of stones overlooked by 'Father Thames' himself sprawling against a bale of wool (this is 'wool country') and a keg or two of brandy: the two commodities remind you that the river leads to the sea, to commerce with countries spread far and wide.

Mason's Trade Marks, Goudhurst, Kent [bottom right]. Facing the north-east corner of the churchyard, with its tomb of Robert Byrne topped by a skull and crossbones dated 1678, is the row of medieval Weavers Cottages; next to them, The Old Lime House, on whose gable-end are three small stone carvings locally known as 'Adam and Eve and the Soup Tureen'. They are 'rubbed work' by a local stone-mason, William Apps, who worked there a century and a half ago and who wished to leave, standing proud from his cottage wall, the symbols of his trade: unbeautiful, perhaps, but an intimate memorial.

It is not surprising that the majority of the Turf-cut Figures to be found in the country are in areas where chalk predominates: Sussex, Berkshire, Wiltshire, parts of Dorset, and the North Riding of Yorkshire. For this reason they are known also as Chalk-cut Figures; and, because they are ordinarily found on hill slopes, they are known also as Hill Figures. Look for them mainly on Downs and Wolds.

A notable display of relatively modern specimens of chalk-cut figures may be seen to the south of A4, on the north slopes of the Wiltshire Downs between Chippenham and Newbury. But these are mainly Regimental Badges and so do not compare in interest with the ancient chalk-out figures such as the famous White Horse of Uffington, Berkshire, between Wantage and Swindon, to the north of this road. Unfortunately this figure, which resembles rather a dismembered dragon than a horse, can be photographed only from the air, for its 374 feet of chalk lines sprawl across a convex slope of thin turf on a hill top, barely visible from the valley road below. No one has yet established with certainty the date when it was first carved out of the turf.

Wilmington Long Man, Sussex, off A27, eight miles north-west of Eastbourne. This mysterious figure sprawls on a north-facing slope of the South Downs known as Windover Hill. He can be photographed (with a telephoto lens) from a vantage-point in a lane passing the ancient Benedictine Priory in Wilmington village. The vantage-point is marked by a stone seat dedicated to the memory of the author, Jeffery Farnol. He holds a stave in each hand, two hundred feet long and rule-straight in spite of the concave slope in which they were cut. Like the White Horse of Uffington, and the equally famous Cerne Giant of Dorset, he is thought to date back to Romano-British times, nearly two thousand years, and to be connected with the war god, Odin. Some think it is not spears that he wields but surveyors' rods, and that he is connected with the laying-out of such ancient trackways as the Berkshire Ridgeway. Certainly his staves lack the fearsome menace of the gnarled bludgeon brandished by his opposite number, the Giant of Cerne on the hill above Cerne Abbas. And unlike him, he has been tactfully emasculated, presumably by the Benedictine monks.

106

MAP SHOWING THE SITES OF ODD ASPECTS
DESCRIBED IN THIS BOOK

KEY

ᐃ FOLLIES
ⵏ WINDMILLS
LOCKUPS
ᵳ PREHISTORIC
R ROMAN REMAINS
✝ MEDIEVAL
✝ MARKET CROSSES AND
   CROSS SHAFTS
● NATURAL FEATURES
□ BUILDINGS
M MEMORIALS
⌐ BRIDGES
★ ODDMENTS

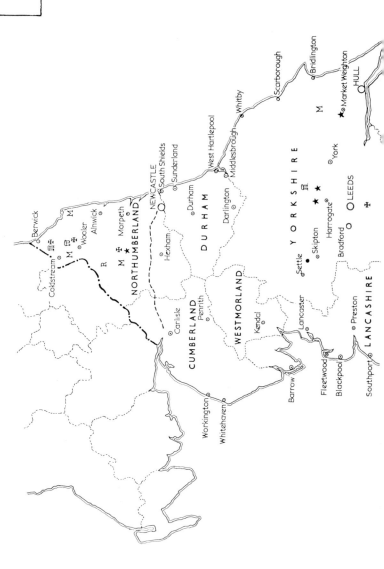

Acknowledgments

I should like particularly to thank Mr R. W. Lavenbein, Chief Librarian of the British Travel Association's Photo Library, and his staff, for their generous assistance in looking out photographs that I required to supplement my own, and for permission to make use of the following: page 39 (top right); page 45 (top left, top right, bottom right); page 65 (top, bottom right); page 69 (top left, bottom left, bottom right); page 73; page 101 (bottom left).

I am indebted also to the Ministry of Public Building and Works for permission to use the photograph on page 11. To the Spa Director, City of Bath, for permission to use the photograph on page 87. And to Mr S. A. Hutchins, of Airport Photo News, Leeds, who supplied the photograph of the Wakefield Bridge Chantry, on page 49.

G.H.

Index (by counties)

Northamptonshire
Eleanor Cross, Geddington, 82
Eleanor Cross, Hardingstone, 82
Triangular Lodge, Rushton, 10

Northumberland
Doddington Pele, 50
Duddo Grooved Monolith, 36
Duddo Pele, 50
Elsdon Pele, 50
Flodden Field Monument, Branxton, 84
Grace Darling Memorial, Bamburgh, 82
Hadrian's Wall, 40
Outer Golden Pot, Chew Green, 44
Percy Stone, Otterburn, 84
Roman Wall, 40
Roughtinglinn Inscribed Stone, 38
Steng Cross Gibbet, 98

Nottinghamshire
Major Oak, Edwinstowe, 66

Oxfordshire
'Carved Hands' Signpost, Wroxton, 104
Chastleton Dove-cote, 52
Witney Butter Cross, 64

Rutland
Oakham Butter Cross, 60

Shropshire
Egyptian Aviary, Tong, 18

Somerset
Batheaston Inn Door, 102
Castle Cary Lock-up, 28
Dunster Yarn Market, 64
Kingsbury Episcopi Lock-up, 28
Pulteney Bridge, Bath, 90
Shepton Mallet Market Cross, 62

Suffolk
Aldeburgh Moot Hall, 78
Dunwich Priory Gateway, 50
Eyke Church Key, 102
Freston (Folly) Tower, 16
House-in-the-Clouds, Thorpeness, 74
Pakenham Tower Mill, 26
Saxstead Green Post Mill, 26

Surrey
Lingfield Lock-up, 30

Sussex
Chichester Market Cross, 56
Long Man of Wilmington, 106
Lullington Church, 78
Shipley Smock Mill, 26
Sugar Loaf, Dallington, 14

Warwickshire
Coleshill Pillory, 100
Cyclists Memorial, Meriden, 84
Edgehill Memorial, Radway, 84
Maxstoke Cruck Cottage, 76
Radway Castle (Folly), Edgehill, 20
Yew Garden, Packwood House, 68

Wiltshire
Collingbourne Ducis Dove-cote, 54
Lacock Cruck Cottage, 76
Malmesbury Market Cross, 58
Oratory Bridge, Bradford-on-Avon, 92
Poultry Cross, Salisbury, 64
Shrewton Lock-up, 30

Yorkshire
Devil's Arrows, Boroughbridge, 34
Malham Cove Clints, 66
Petrifying Well, Knaresborough, 104
Ripley Stocks, 100
Sundial Cottage, Seaton Ross, 102
Waggoners Memorial, Sledmere, 82
Wakefield Bridge Chantry, 48